a good day to bake

Simple Baking Recipes
for Every Mood

Photography by Laura Edwards

Benjamina Ebuehi

Hardie Grant

QUADRILLE

Recipe notes

Ingredients are listed using British terms and metric measurements first, followed by US terms and imperial/cup measurements in brackets. Please follow one system of measurement when following the recipes.

All eggs used are large and given in UK sizes. Readers in the US should go up a size. All milk used is full-fat.

introduction

I'm not someone who needs an excuse to bake. Being able
to whip out my mixer and hide away in the kitchen for
an afternoon or evening, just to satisfy a sweet craving,
is something that my mum still can't get her head around.
Setting aside a little time during the week to use my hands
to create something that will bring a smile to people's faces
and joy to their bellies is an act I don't take for granted.
Going through the ritual of bringing out my measuring scales,
pouring out flour, whipping up eggs, stirring the batter and
impatiently slicing up warm cake is a beautiful thing that
deserves to be enjoyed all year round, no matter the day,
season or occasion.

A slice of flourless chocolate cake, a batch of miso cookies
or a herb-infused custard tart can brighten up the dreariest
of Mondays and a little creativity each day goes a long way.
I wrote most of this book during a strange time of lockdowns
and the world being flipped on its head. One small joy was
seeing how many people picked up baking for the first time or
returned to it after some time away. Watching and being a part
of people discovering just how therapeutic and comforting
baking can be was quite special. Whether it was baking just
to pass the time, baking with kids to keep them busy while
home schooling, or providing homemade goodies to frontline
workers, it was a sweet reminder of the way that food really
does bring us together. I'd get messages explaining how excited
someone was that they were able to nail a new technique for
the first time or just enjoying the fact that they could slow
down a bit and take pleasure in the act of making a cake.
It looked as though we were all willing to enjoy the process
that little bit more, regardless of what the outcome would be.
More than ever, I find myself appreciating the little things and
taking more time to celebrate those small daily wins alongside
the big ones, and I love that I can do that through food.

I want this book to help us all remember and hold on to those
moments of pause. Every day could do with a bit more slowing
down, a little more stirring, kneading, folding and peering
into the oven watching bread puff up like magic. More than
what the end result looks like, the route to get there can be

just as fulfilling. There's often a moment in most recipes where I have a little pause to take it all in. It could be that split second just before you pour ganache over your chocolate cake, or smoothing the batter in the pan right before it goes in the oven. It could be that fleeting moment where you feel the full weight of your knife as it sinks into your cake for the first slice, or the few seconds you take to admire the sheer volume and silkiness of your meringue. It's those brief but meaningful steps of a recipe that are unwritten but can feel the most rewarding. The moments that make you say, 'Yes, I'm doing this right. And this feels good.'

The recipes in this book are approachable, simple in appearance and, above all, full of flavour. Rather than focusing on really intricate and fanciful decoration, I've tried to celebrate the ingredients by having them front and centre with almost nowhere to hide. The Herbs and Tea chapter makes the most of nature's best, with ingredients like hibiscus, mint, matcha, rosemary and tarragon. Stone Fruit and Berries brings together the colourful and juicy offerings of summer. The Vegetable chapter highlights the versatility of root veg in baking, while the Best of Beige is a pure celebration of the comforting nature of beige and brown food. Spice Cupboard shows you just how easy it is to transform a bake with spices such as nutmeg, cardamom or za'atar. And I don't think I could ever write a cookbook without a Chocolate chapter.

Each day comes with its own mood, cravings and needs, and I hope there's a recipe for you to turn to no matter how your day is going. There'll be days where you need a recipe that's more hands-on and requires all of you – it might be the rice pudding that asks for your undivided attention while stirring or the custard tart that needs a watchful eye so it doesn't overbake. And there'll be days when time is of the essence, but you need something to satisfy now. It can be so easy to get lost and caught up in the rhythms of the week, but let the kitchen – however big or small – be a space in which you let loose, slow down and are present. Because every day is a good day to bake.

herbs & tea

Go into most kitchens and I'm pretty sure you'll be able to open a cupboard and stumble across a decent selection of teas – most likely an English breakfast, an Earl Grey or a herbal offering, if you're lucky. A quick rummage in the refrigerator is likely to uncover a couple of packets of fresh herbs, perhaps looking a little sad, waiting to get used in a dinner that week. Herbs and teas are such staple and loyal members of our kitchens, yet don't always get a look in when it comes to baking.

Both items provide such easy and effective ways to infuse flavour and bring in more delicate, complex notes to custards, cakes, breads and desserts, whether it's the liquorice notes of tarragon embedded into blondies, or the bright, floral buds of chamomile that sing when infused into a syrup for chamomile lemon buns. And what beautiful colours they bring! The striking purple of hibiscus and the grassy colour of matcha both bring a bit of nature indoors.

In the way that making a good cup of tea can be quite a ritual – soothing and familiar – baking with it can provide a similar level of calm. If you've got loose leaf tea, then you'll get some of the best aromatic and flavourful infusions, but I often just opt for loose leaf tea bags, which I find a bit more convenient to store.

chamomile lemon buns

Sticky buns are the best buns. There's a quiet joy in unravelling a soft, squishy bun, eating it layer by layer, making it last as long as possible. These delicately fragranced, pillowy rolls are no exception, and you get the added bonus of a sweet sticky bottom as the lemony sugar caramelizes in the pan. I know I say let them cool completely before serving, but I won't blame you if you jump in as soon as they're cool enough to handle.

Makes 7 buns

150ml (5fl oz/scant ⅔ cup) milk

4 loose leaf chamomile tea bags

1 tsp vanilla bean paste

300g (10½oz/generous 2 cups) strong bread flour, plus extra for dusting

25g (1oz/3 Tbsp) caster (granulated) sugar

½ tsp fine sea salt

1 tsp fast-action dried yeast

1 egg, beaten

25g (1½ Tbsp) unsalted butter, softened, plus extra for greasing

1 Tbsp pearl sugar (optional)

For the filling

100g (3½oz/½ cup) caster (granulated) sugar

grated zest of 2 lemons

85g (3oz/⅓ cup plus 2 tsp) unsalted butter, softened

For the syrup

100ml (3½fl oz/scant ½ cup) water

100g (3½oz/½ cup) caster (granulated) sugar

2 chamomile tea bags

Add the milk, tea bags and vanilla to a medium saucepan and bring to a gentle simmer. Once heated through, remove from the heat, cover and let the milk steep and cool for 30 minutes. Strain the milk into a jug (pitcher), squeezing the tea bags, then set aside.

In a large bowl or the bowl of a stand mixer, mix together the flour and sugar. Add in the salt and yeast to separate sides of the bowl, make a well in the centre and pour in the beaten egg and cooled milk. If using a stand mixer fitted with a dough hook, mix for 6 minutes on low speed. If mixing by hand, knead in the bowl for 10 minutes (the dough will be quite sticky at first, but try not to add too much extra flour). Let the dough rest, uncovered, for 5 minutes, then knead for a further 4 minutes until you have a smooth dough. Add the softened butter and knead for a further 5 minutes until you have a shiny, supple dough.

Place the dough into a lightly greased bowl, cover with plastic wrap or a clean dish towel and leave to prove in a warm place for 1–2 hours or until nearly doubled in size.

Meanwhile, make the filling. Mix the caster sugar and lemon zest together in a bowl, using your fingertips to rub the zest into the sugar until it resembles wet sand. Add the softened butter and mix until thoroughly combined. Set aside.

Preheat the oven to 200°C (180°C fan/400°F/gas mark 6). Line the base of a 20-cm (8-in) springform or loose-bottomed cake pan with baking paper and grease the sides.

Once the dough has risen, use your fingertips to press it down and knock the air back. Turn it out onto a lightly floured surface and roll it into a large rectangle, about 3–4mm (⅛in) thick. Spread the filling mixture evenly across the surface. Starting from one of the longest sides, roll the dough up tightly and slice into 7 equal rolls. Arrange the rolls in the prepared pan, leaving a bit of space between them, and cover the pan loosely with a dish towel. Leave to prove for 25–35 minutes, or until the rolls are puffy and touching each other.

Top with pearl sugar, if using, and bake for 35–40 minutes until a deep brown colour.

While the buns bake, make the syrup. Add the water, sugar and tea bags to a small saucepan, bring to the boil and let simmer for 1 minute. Remove from the heat and set aside.

When the buns are baked, let them cool for a few minutes before brushing them generously with the chamomile syrup, letting it seep through. Let them cool completely before serving.

rosemary & honey scones

It's hard to beat a fresh scone, still a little warm from the oven, smeared in clotted cream and devoured before you've had a chance to put the kettle on. Scones are my go-to when I'm short on time. Relying on store-cupboard basics, you're likely to already have everything to hand, allowing you to throw these together as soon the craving hits. The flecks of rosemary running through these add a warm, piney aroma that makes them feel a little fancy without doing much.

Makes 4

450g (1lb/scant 3½ cups) plain (all-purpose) flour, plus extra for dusting

1 Tbsp baking powder

40g (1½oz/3¼ Tbsp) caster (granulated) sugar

¼ tsp salt

220g (7¾oz/1 cup) cold unsalted butter, diced

1½ Tbsp finely chopped rosemary

130ml (4½fl oz/generous ½ cup) milk

1 egg

1½ tsp honey

For the glaze

2 Tbsp honey

3 Tbsp water

2 sprigs of rosemary

To serve

salted butter or clotted cream

honey, for drizzling

Preheat the oven to 200°C (180°C fan/400°F/gas mark 6). Line two baking sheets with baking paper.

In a large bowl, mix together the flour, baking powder, sugar and salt. Add in the butter and toss in the flour to coat. Rub the mixture between your fingertips until it resembles coarse breadcrumbs. Add the chopped rosemary and stir.

In a jug (pitcher), whisk together the milk, egg and honey. Make a well in the centre of the flour mixture and pour in the liquid, using a knife to stir until it begins to clump together and you have a soft dough.

Turn the dough out onto a lightly floured surface and knead very gently and briefly, folding the dough back on itself a couple of times – the surface doesn't need to be perfectly smooth, so try not to overwork it.

Pat the dough into a thick, round disc and slice into 8 wedges. Place the wedges on the baking sheets, leaving about 2.5cm (1in) between them.

Bake for 16–20 minutes or until well risen and golden.

To make the glaze, gently heat the honey, water and rosemary sprigs together in a small pan. Bring the mixture to the boil and boil for 1 minute, then brush directly over the warm scones.

Serve with salted butter or clotted cream and an extra little drizzle of honey.

HERBS & TEA

hibiscus mint granita
with salted butter biscuits

The colour of hibiscus always draws me in. Rich and deep, it's easy to get a little lost in the dark cherry hues of the slushy crystals, as you go back and forth to give it a scrape. Granita is such a refreshing treat – it instantly transports me to lazy sunny afternoons on holiday, the soft ice melting faster than you can eat it. I serve these with little, salty, buttery biscuits because I'm a sucker for some extra crunch.

Serves 4–6

250ml (9fl oz/generous 1 cup) freshly boiled water
30g (1oz/5 Tbsp) loose leaf hibiscus tea
juice of ½ lime

For the sugar syrup
70g (2½oz/⅓ cup) caster (granulated) sugar
70ml (2¼fl oz/4½ Tbsp) water
6 mint leaves, finely chopped

For the salted butter biscuits
50g (1¾oz/3½ Tbsp) salted butter
45g (1½oz/¼ cup) caster (granulated) sugar
1 egg yolk
85g (3oz/⅔ cup) plain (all-purpose) flour
flaky sea salt, for sprinkling

Measure out the boiled water into a jug (pitcher) and let it cool for a couple of minutes. Add the hibiscus tea leaves, stir, and leave to steep for 20 minutes. Strain the tea and discard the leaves.

To make the syrup, in a small saucepan, heat the sugar and water until the sugar has completely dissolved. Stir in the mint leaves and let the syrup cool.

Pour the cooled syrup into the tea along with the lime juice. At this point give it a taste, adding more lime juice if you prefer more acidity. Pour the mixture into a large, shallow container with a lid and let it cool to room temperature.

Transfer the container to the freezer and freeze for 1 hour, then use a fork to agitate the mixture, scraping down the sides and breaking down any clumps. Freeze for another 30 minutes. Repeat this freezing and agitating process every 30–45 minutes until you have a slushy mixture.

To make the biscuits, beat the butter and sugar together in a bowl until creamy. (You can do this by hand with a wooden spoon.) Beat in the egg yolk, then mix in the flour to give you a thick dough. Wrap the dough in plastic wrap and chill for 1 hour.

Preheat the oven to 180°C (160°C fan/350°F/gas mark 4). Line two baking sheets with baking paper.

Divide the dough into 12–14 small balls and place them on the baking sheets, leaving plenty of space between them. Flatten the tops with your fingertips. Bake for 10–12 minutes, turning the sheets around halfway through, until the biscuits just start to brown on the edges. Remove from the oven and top the biscuits with a little flaky sea salt. Leave to cool completely.

When ready to serve, scrape the granita with a fork and spoon into small glasses or ramekins. Serve with the biscuits.

earl grey, orange & white chocolate traybake

Earl Grey is my go-to tea for that 3-o'clock pick me up, and is always accompanied with a little slice of something sweet. So, having the tea steeped into the cake kind of kills two birds with one stone. It's floral and citrussy with a soft delicate crumb, extra orange zest complements the bergamot notes in the tea, and it's all topped off with a creamy, white chocolate buttercream. For the days where a cup of tea alone doesn't quite cut it, this is the cake to make.

Serves 12 (for a smaller, 20-cm/8-in square cake, split the recipe in half)

For the peaches
220ml (7½fl oz/scant 1 cup) milk

3 good-quality Earl Grey tea bags

120g (4¼oz/½ cup) unsalted butter

1 tsp vanilla extract

4 eggs

280g (10oz/scant 1½ cups) caster (granulated) sugar

grated zest of 1½ oranges

280g (10oz/generous 2 cups) plain (all-purpose) flour

2 tsp baking powder

For the syrup
juice of 1 orange

30g (1oz/2½ Tbsp) caster (granulated) sugar

1 Earl Grey teabag

For the buttercream frosting
175g (6oz/¾ cup) unsalted butter, softened

130g (4½oz/scant 1 cup) icing (confectioners') sugar

¼ tsp salt

120g (4¼oz) white chocolate, melted, plus extra shavings

flaked (slivered) almonds and dried cornflowers (optional)

Preheat the oven to 180°C (160°C fan/350°F/gas mark 4). Grease a 23 x 33-cm (9 x 13-in) sheet pan and line with baking paper, leaving an overhang to help you lift the sponge out later.

In a small saucepan, gently heat the milk, tea bags, butter and vanilla until just before the boil. Remove from the heat, cover and let the milk steep and cool for 15 minutes.

In the bowl of a stand mixer, whisk the eggs, sugar and two-thirds of the orange zest on high speed for 4–6 minutes or until the eggs are thick, pale and nearly doubled in volume.

Remove the tea bags from the cooled milk and with the mixer still running, pour the milk slowly into the eggs. Add the flour and baking powder and beat until you have a smooth, runny batter.

Pour the batter into the prepared pan and bake for 35–38 minutes, or until a skewer inserted into the centre comes out clean.

While the cake bakes, make the syrup. Heat the orange juice, sugar and tea bag in a small saucepan and bring to the boil. Let it simmer for 1 minute before removing from the heat.

While the cake is still warm, prick the surface with a skewer and pour the syrup over the cake, then set aside to cool completely.

To make the buttercream frosting, beat the butter in the stand mixer on high speed for 2 minutes until creamy. Add the icing sugar and salt and beat for a further 4–6 minutes until you have a pale, fluffy buttercream. Pour in the melted chocolate and beat for another minute until combined.

Spread the frosting evenly on top of the cake, using a palette knife to either smooth it over or to add some texture. Top with the remaining orange zest, white chocolate shavings, flaked almonds, and dried cornflowers, if using, before slicing up.

HERBS & TEA

chive, tarragon & dill sesame twists

Inspired by Turkish simit, these twists are filled with a beautiful combination of herbs held inside a toasty, sesame crust. You can switch up the herbs used here, depending on what you've got lying around – just don't hold back. For the perfect start to your weekend or to perk up your Monday morning, slice these up, slather with cream cheese and top with some smoked salmon.

Makes 6

450g (1lb/3¼ cups) strong white bread flour, plus extra for dusting

1 tsp salt

2 tsp fast-action dried yeast

2 Tbsp each of chives, tarragon and dill, finely chopped

240ml (8fl oz/1 cup) lukewarm water

3 Tbsp olive oil, plus extra for greasing

To coat

1 Tbsp honey

100ml (3½fl oz/scant ½ cup) lukewarm water

100g (3½oz/⅔ cup) sesame seeds

Add the flour to a large mixing bowl, then add the salt and yeast to separate sides of the bowl so they're not directly touching. Mix together and then stir in the herbs. Make a well in the centre and pour in the water along with the oil. Stir together to form a shaggy dough.

Turn the dough out onto a lightly floured work surface and knead for 6–8 minutes until smooth and elastic. Place the dough in a lightly greased bowl, cover and leave to prove in a warm place for 1–2 hours, or until nearly doubled in size.

Once risen, knock out the air and turn the dough out onto a clean work surface. Divide the dough into 6 equal pieces. Split each piece in half and roll each into a long sausage, about 60cm (24in) long. Twist the two strands together and bring the ends together to make a loop, pinching where they meet to seal. Repeat with the rest of the dough pieces.

Line a large baking sheet with baking paper. In a shallow dish, mix the honey with the lukewarm water. Add the sesame seeds to a separate shallow dish.

Dip each twist in the honey water and then into the sesame seeds, making sure they're properly coated. Place the twists on the prepared baking sheet, cover with plastic wrap and let them prove for another 20–30 minutes until puffy.

Meanwhile, preheat the oven to 200°C (180°C fan/400°F/gas mark 6).

Bake the twists for 18–22 minutes until golden. Let them cool completely before serving.

matcha & lemon posset tarts

Their colour might imply 'healthy', but don't let that fool you. Cream is the main ingredient in this tart filling and I'm very much here for it. The earthy grassiness of matcha can be a bit divisive but I just can't get enough of it. This is such a simple little pudding that comes together in no time, ideal for a make-ahead dessert that doesn't require too much effort.

Serves 5

For the pastry

95g (3⅓oz/⅓ cup plus 1 Tbsp) cold unsalted butter, cubed

50g (1¾oz/generous ⅓ cup) icing (confectioners') sugar

1 tsp vanilla bean paste

2 egg yolks

190g (6¾oz/scant 1½ cups) plain (all-purpose) flour, plus extra for dusting

¼ tsp salt

For the filling

100g (3½oz/½ cup) caster (granulated) sugar

grated zest of 1 lemon

3 Tbsp lemon juice (from about 1–1½ lemons)

2½ tsp matcha, plus extra for dusting

300ml (10½fl oz/generous 1¼ cups) double (heavy) cream

To make the pastry, beat the butter, sugar and vanilla together by hand or with an electric whisk until you have a smooth, thick paste. Add the egg yolks and beat until smooth, scraping down the sides of the bowl every so often. Add the flour and salt and mix briefly on low speed until just combined. Tip the dough onto a sheet of plastic wrap and pat it into a thick rectangle. Wrap it up and chill in the refrigerator for 1 hour or until firm.

Get five 8-cm (3-in) round tart pans ready; there's no need to grease them. Lightly flour your work surface and roll the pastry out to 3–4mm (⅛in) thick. Cut out 5 circles a few centimetres wider than your tart pans. Press each piece into the pans, making sure to press the dough into the edges or corners and leaving the excess pastry overhanging the edges. Place the tart pans on a baking sheet and refrigerate for 20 minutes. Meanwhile, preheat the oven to 180°C (160°C fan/350°F/gas mark 4).

Once chilled, trim off the overhanging pastry with a sharp knife and prick the bases with a fork. Scrunch up pieces of baking paper slightly larger than the pans and place them inside, pressing the paper into all the corners. Fill with dried rice or baking beans and blind bake for 12–15 minutes until the edges are lightly golden.

Remove the paper and baking beans and return the tart cases to the oven for a further 10–12 minutes until golden. Leave to cool.

To make the filling, gently heat the sugar, lemon zest and juice in a small saucepan. Bring to a simmer until the sugar dissolves. Add the matcha to a small bowl and mix in about 1 tablespoon of the lemon syrup. Mix thoroughly to get a thick paste before adding another couple of tablespoons of syrup and mixing well – use a bamboo matcha whisk if you have one to help dissolve most of the smaller lumps. Pour in the rest of the syrup and set aside.

In another saucepan, gently bring the cream to the boil, stirring often. Pour in the matcha syrup and whisk well to mix. Remove from the heat and pour the mixture through a sieve (strainer) to get rid of any stray lumps. Fill the cooled tart cases with the mixture and let them cool at room temperature before chilling for 2–3 hours until set. Dust with a little extra matcha before serving.

sour cream sage doughnuts

These are based on the old-fashioned, sour cream doughnuts I would buy multiple times a week as an exchange student in Canada. The dense, cakey interior and signature scraggly crust are completely opposite to a more traditional yeasted doughnut, but these always draw me in again and again. I've flavoured them with sage, one of my favourite herbs, which often doesn't get much use outside of the Christmas table. However, it works so well in sweet recipes, bringing an aromatic, earthy tone.

Makes 8–10 doughnuts plus doughnut holes

300g (10½oz/2¼ cups) plain (all-purpose) flour, plus extra for dusting

1 Tbsp cornflour (cornstarch)

2 tsp baking powder

½ tsp salt

120g (4¼oz/scant ⅔ cup) caster (granulated) sugar

16 fresh sage leaves, finely chopped

3 egg yolks

20g (1½ Tbsp) unsalted butter, softened

150g (5½oz/scant ¾ cup) sour cream

1 litre (35fl oz/4 cups) vegetable oil, for deep-frying

For the glaze

250g (9oz/1¾ cups) icing (confectioners') sugar

50ml (2fl oz/3½ Tbsp) milk, plus more if needed

1 tsp vanilla extract

pinch of salt

Mix the flour, cornflour, baking powder and salt together in a small bowl and set aside.

In a large bowl, add the sugar and sage. Use your fingertips to rub the sage into the sugar until fragrant. Add the yolks and butter to the bowl and whip together until pale and smooth. Pour in the sour cream and beat for another minute to combine.

Add the flour mixture in 3 batches, stirring gently after each addition. Once all the flour has been added, wrap the dough in plastic wrap – it'll be quite soft and a little sticky. Chill in the refrigerator for 1–2 hours, or until it has firmed up. (You can also make this ahead and leave the dough in the refrigerator overnight.)

Once chilled, generously dust your work surface with flour. Roll the dough out to about 1cm (½in) thick. Dip a doughnut cutter in some flour and cut out as many doughnuts and doughnut holes as you can before re-rolling and cutting again. Place the doughnuts on a baking sheet to chill in the refrigerator.

Pour a 5cm (2in) depth of oil into a heavy-based saucepan (or use a deep-fat fryer) and heat to 170°C (340°F) or until a cube of bread sizzles and browns when dropped into the hot oil. Fry 2–3 doughnuts at a time, for about 2 minutes on each side, keeping an eye on the temperature of the oil and adjusting the heat when necessary. The doughnut holes will take about half the time to cook. Place the cooked doughnuts on a plate lined with paper towels to soak up excess oil and let them cool for a few minutes.

To make the glaze, add all the ingredients to a bowl and whisk until smooth. The glaze should be quite runny, so add a little more milk if it's too thick. Dip the doughnut holes and the top of each doughnut quickly in the glaze and place them on a wire rack with a tray underneath to catch the drips. Let the glaze set for 15 minutes before serving.

HERBS & TEA

thyme-sugar churros

Without fail, churros transport me to memories of being on holiday. After a day of traipsing up and down a new city, there's a particular time late into the afternoon when a good sugar boost is needed, and somehow your nose manages to guide you to that sweet, familiar, fried dough smell. Grinding the thyme into the sugar is an easy way of bringing more fragrance to these churros, brightening them up and making them interesting enough to serve without a dipping sauce. Deep frying can feel a little intimidating sometimes, so just take it easy. If you're not confident to pipe the dough directly into the oil, you can pipe shapes onto small pieces of baking paper first.

Serves 6

200ml (7fl oz/scant 1 cup) water

75g (2½oz/⅓ cup) salted butter

grated zest of 1 lemon

2 tsp caster (granulated) sugar

160g (5¾oz/scant 1¼ cups) plain (all-purpose) flour

3 eggs

1 litre (35fl oz/4 cups) vegetable oil, for deep-frying

For the thyme sugar

150g (5½oz/¾ cup) caster (granulated) sugar

2 Tbsp fresh thyme leaves

First, make the thyme sugar. Grind the sugar and thyme leaves with a pestle and mortar until fragrant, then pour into a shallow dish and set aside. Alternatively, just rub the thyme into the sugar with your fingertips until it resembles wet sand.

To make the churros, heat the water, butter, lemon zest and 2 tsp sugar in a medium saucepan and bring to the boil. Pour in the flour all at once while stirring continuously. It'll be lumpy at first, but keep mixing until you have a thick, smooth ball of dough. Turn the heat down and continue to cook the dough for 1 minute, stirring continuously. Remove from the heat and put the dough into a clean bowl to cool for about 5 minutes.

Crack the eggs into a jug or cup and gently beat with a fork. Pour the eggs into the dough a little at a time, beating well after each addition. The dough will look as though it's not coming together at first, but keep mixing and it'll begin to combine. You may not need to use all of the eggs – you're looking for a consistency that is thick enough to pipe and will slowly fall off a spoon after a few seconds.

Heat a 10cm (4in) depth of oil in a medium, heavy-based saucepan (or use a deep-fat fryer) to 170°C (340°F). If you don't have a thermometer, test a little bit of the dough – it should sizzle and float quite quickly and take about 30–60 seconds to brown. If it darkens quickly but is still raw in the middle, turn down the heat.

Spoon the dough into a piping bag fitted with a large open star nozzle (I use Wilton 1M). Once the oil is at temperature, hold your piping bag directly over the oil and pipe in a strip of dough 8–10cm (3–4in) long. Use a pair of clean scissors to snip off the end, letting the dough float into the oil. Repeat until you have 3–4 churros in the pan. Let them fry for 1–2 minutes on each side until they're puffy and golden. Use tongs to remove them from the oil, placing them on a plate lined with paper towels.

Toss the still-warm churros in the thyme sugar and serve.

bay leaf custard tart

There are quite a few custard-based recipes in this book, such is my love for the stuff in all of its glorious forms. And nothing quite beats a classic custard tart. Just infusing the cream with a few fresh bay leaves transforms this into something quite fragrant and almost tea-like. Bay leaves are an ingredient that tends to get thrown into a stew or soup without knowing what it actually tastes like. It's not necessarily a flavour a lot of people could identify on its own. But here, woven into the silky custard, it sings. Fresh bay is a must here to really get the best flavour.

Serves 8

For the pastry

210g (7½oz/1½ cups) plain (all-purpose) flour, plus extra for dusting

60g (2¼oz/scant ½ cup) icing (confectioners') sugar

¼ tsp salt

130g (4¾oz/½ cup plus 1 Tbsp) unsalted butter

1 egg, separated

2–3 Tbsp ice-cold water

For the custard

250ml (9fl oz/generous 1 cup) milk

300ml (10½fl oz/generous 1¼ cups) double (heavy) cream

8 fresh bay leaves

7 egg yolks

100g (3½oz/½ cup) caster (granulated) sugar

Add the flour, icing sugar, salt and butter to the bowl of a food processor and pulse until you have fine breadcrumbs. (If making by hand, rub the butter into the flour until fine.) Add the egg yolk and a tablespoon of ice-cold water and pulse until it starts to clump, adding more water, a tablespoon at a time, if needed.

Turn the dough out onto a lightly floured surface and pat it into a thick disc. Wrap it in plastic wrap and let it rest in the refrigerator for 1 hour, or until well chilled and firm.

Meanwhile, make the custard. Add the milk, cream and bay leaves to a small saucepan and heat gently until steaming, just before the boil. Remove from the heat, cover and let the cream infuse for 30 minutes–1 hour.

Preheat the oven to 190°C (170°C fan/375°F/gas mark 5).

Lightly dust your work surface with flour and roll out the pastry to 3–4mm (⅛in) thick. Line a 20-cm (8-in) tart pan or loose-bottomed cake pan with the pastry, making sure to press the pastry evenly into the edges and leaving an overhang of pastry around the rim. Prick the base of the pastry a few times with a fork, then pop it in the freezer for 15 minutes.

Once chilled, use a small, sharp knife to trim off the overhanging pastry to give a neat crust. Scrunch up a piece of baking paper, open it out again and use it to line the inside of the tart. Fill with baking beans or uncooked rice and blind bake for 20 minutes.

Carefully remove the baking beans and paper and continue to bake for another 15–22 minutes, until the edges have browned and the base is firm to the touch. Brush the base with a little bit of the egg white and put back in the oven for 2 minutes – this will help create a seal for the custard. Remove from the oven and leave to cool.

Reduce the oven to 150°C (130°C fan/300°F/gas mark 2).

To finish the custard, in a separate bowl, whisk the egg yolks and sugar together until combined.

Strain the bay leaves from the saucepan and return the cream to the pan. Gently bring to the boil.

Pour the hot cream into the egg mixture, whisking to combine, then pass the custard through a fine sieve (strainer) to catch any little lumps.

Pour half of the custard into the pastry shell and skim off and discard any foam on the top. Place the tart on a baking sheet and into the oven. Pour in the rest of the custard and bake for 30–40 minutes until just set with a jelly-like wobble in the middle. Remove from the oven and leave to cool completely.

Serve at room temperature or chilled.

tarragon blondies

When you think of tarragon, what comes to mind? It's not the most used or popular herb and, likewise, blondies tend to be outshone by their more popular big sister, the brownie. So these two are right at home together, creating something deliciously unexpected. The liquorice flavour of the tarragon comes through subtly and sits comfortably against the buttery sweetness of the blondies. Laying the leaves on top of the batter, right before it goes into the oven, is my favourite bit when making these. I enjoy the process of laying them down, and letting them overlap, curl and bend in any which way they fancy.

Makes 9–12

225g (8oz/1 cup) unsalted butter, plus extra for greasing

5 sprigs of tarragon, plus extra leaves to decorate

200g (7oz/1 cup) light brown sugar

2 eggs

1 tsp vanilla bean paste

160g (5¾oz/scant 1¼ cups) plain (all-purpose) flour

pinch of ground cloves

½ tsp salt

100g (3½oz) white chocolate, roughly chopped

50g (2oz/⅓ cup) macadamia nuts, roughly chopped

Preheat the oven to 180°C (160°C fan/350°F/gas mark 4). Grease and line a 20-cm (8-in) square cake pan.

Finely chop one sprig of tarragon and set aside.

Add the butter and remaining 4 whole sprigs of tarragon to a small saucepan. Gently melt the butter, then remove from the heat, cover and let it steep for 15–20 minutes. (For a stronger flavour you can leave this for 1 hour.)

Strain the butter into a large bowl, discarding the herbs. Once cooled, mix in the sugar, then stir in the eggs and vanilla until smooth. Add the flour, ground cloves, chopped tarragon and salt, stirring gently until just combined. Mix in the white chocolate and chopped nuts.

Pour the batter into the prepared pan and arrange the extra tarragon leaves on top of the batter. Bake for 20–25 minutes or until just set.

Let the blondies cool completely before serving. For a super clean cut, chill them in the refrigerator for a few hours before slicing with a sharp knife.

HERBS & TEA

mint & lemon drizzle cake

A classic lemon drizzle is pretty hard to beat. Whatever the weather, season or mood, I will choose this cake again and again. It's got the perfect balance of sweet and sharp, and a soft, buttery crumb that gets drenched in lemony syrup. This version is still all of those things but with some extra brightness and fragrance from a good handful of fresh mint. It's such a simple twist but wins big on the flavour front, giving you a cake that'll feel right at home at any time of any day.

Serves 8–10

200g (7oz/¾ cup plus 2 Tbsp) unsalted butter, plus extra for greasing

250g (9oz/1¼ cups) caster (granulated) sugar

10g (¼oz) fresh mint leaves, plus extra to decorate

finely grated zest of 2 lemons

3 eggs

270g (9½oz/2 cups) plain (all-purpose) flour

1½ tsp baking powder

¼ tsp salt

2 Tbsp milk

For the syrup

50g (1¾oz/1¼ cups) caster (granulated) sugar

juice of 2 lemons

3 fresh mint leaves

For the frosting

70g (2½oz/½ cup) icing (confectioners') sugar

2–3 Tbsp lemon juice (from about 1 lemon)

Preheat the oven to 180°C (160°C fan/350°F/gas mark 4). Grease and line a 900-g (2-lb) loaf pan.

Add the sugar and mint to a food processor and blitz until the mint is finely chopped.

Cream the butter, minty sugar and lemon zest together with an electric whisk for 3–5 minutes until really pale and fluffy. Add the eggs, one at a time, beating well after each addition. Tip in the flour, baking powder and salt and mix on low speed until smooth. Finally, stir in the milk.

Pour the batter into the prepared pan and smooth the top. Bake for 50–60 minutes until golden and a skewer inserted into the middle of the cake comes out clean.

Meanwhile, make the syrup. Heat the sugar, lemon juice and mint in a small saucepan until the sugar dissolves. Let it simmer for 1 minute before removing from the heat.

When the cake is out of the oven, use a skewer or toothpick to prick the whole surface. Pour the syrup on top, letting it seep into the holes. Let the cake cool completely in the pan.

Make the frosting by mixing the icing sugar and lemon juice together until you have a thick but pourable consistency. If it looks too thin, just add a little more icing sugar; if you want to thin it out, stir in a bit more lemon juice.

Remove the cooled cake from the pan and pour the frosting on top, letting it drip down the sides. Top with a couple of small mint leaves before serving.

rooibos & rose friands

Friands are such pretty little cakes that look really fancy but are actually incredibly easy to make. Infusing the butter with rooibos tea brings a warm, earthy sweetness to these almond cakes that even the strongest rooibos haters will be able to appreciate. I've paired it with some rosewater for a delicate floral touch, making these so perfect for a little springtime afternoon tea. You can bake these in a classic oval friand pan, or if – like me – you're trying not to purchase yet another cake pan, these work perfectly in a small muffin pan or cupcake tray.

Makes 8–10

150g (5½oz/⅔ cup) unsalted butter, plus extra for greasing

40g (1½oz/generous ¼ cup) plain (all-purpose) flour, plus extra for dusting

2 Tbsp loose leaf rooibos tea

200g (7oz/scant 1½ cups) icing (confectioners') sugar, plus extra for dusting

110g (3¾oz/generous 1 cup) ground almonds

¼ tsp salt

200g (7oz) egg whites

1 tsp vanilla bean paste

½ tsp rosewater

2½ Tbsp flaked (slivered) almonds

dried rose petals, to decorate

Preheat the oven to 210°C (190°C fan/400°F/gas mark 6). Grease a muffin or friand pan with some melted butter and sprinkle the holes with a little flour, tapping it around to make sure it's evenly coated. Tap out the excess and set aside.

Add the butter and tea to a small saucepan and heat gently until the butter has melted. Let the butter cool and infuse for 10 minutes, then strain out and discard the tea leaves through a fine mesh sieve (strainer).

In a large bowl, combine the flour, icing sugar, ground almonds and salt.

In a separate bowl, whisk together the egg whites, vanilla and rosewater until frothy. You're not looking for soft peaks here, so this will only take a few seconds. Pour the egg whites into the dry ingredients and stir until combined, then mix in the infused butter.

Pour the batter evenly into the holes of the prepared pan and top each one with flaked almonds. Bake for 20–25 minutes, turning the tray around halfway through, until golden and a skewer inserted into the middle of a cake comes out clean.

Leave to cool in the pan for a few minutes before removing to a wire rack to cool completely. Once cooled, dust with icing sugar and top with some dried rose petals.

stone fruit
& berries

This chapter really is an ode to summer. Bright, fresh mornings, steady streams of sunlight, afternoons spent outside with family and friends, and long summer evenings, laughing and eating well into the night. My memories of summers gone by revolve around big fruity puddings, sticky, sweet and refreshing. Big pavlovas to share, bubbling cobblers with scoops of ice cream, and cakes generously sandwiched with berries and cream. The most beautiful, vibrant colours, all coming together on my plate, just fill me with joy.

A lot of these recipes can be made with both fresh or frozen fruit, allowing you to make the most of the summer bounty for most of the year. You can use frozen fruit straight from the freezer without needing to defrost it, unless otherwise stated in the recipe. Many of the recipes are interchangeable too – you can use apricots instead of nectarines on the focaccia or blueberries instead of blackberries in the blackberry and sage pudding.

blackberry & sage pudding

This is a sort of cake/pudding hybrid, made up of an oozy, bubbling layer of blackberries, lightly fragranced with sage, baked in between a soft, buttery sponge. Liberally topped with flaked almonds and demerara sugar, the crisp top gives way to the fruit wanting to break through underneath. I tend to make this as a bit of a last hurrah to summer, as blackberries in the UK are at their best just as we start to head into the cooler autumn months.

Serves 6

2 Tbsp unsalted butter, plus extra for greasing

250g (9oz) fresh or frozen blackberries

3 Tbsp caster (granulated) sugar

12 sage leaves, finely chopped

zest of 1 lemon

For the sponge

130g (4½oz/½ cup plus 1 Tbsp) unsalted butter

160g (5¾oz/scant 1¼ cups) plain (all-purpose) flour

175g (6oz/¾ cup plus 2 Tbsp) caster (granulated) sugar

1½ tsp baking powder

¼ tsp salt

50g (1¾oz/½ cup) ground almonds

2 eggs

1 tsp vanilla bean paste or extract

3 Tbsp double (heavy) cream

50g (1¾oz/⅔ cup) flaked (slivered) almonds

2 tsp demerara (turbinado) sugar

To serve

cream or ice cream

Preheat the oven to 180°C (160°C fan/350°F/gas mark 4) and lightly grease a baking dish approximately 26 x 21cm (10¼ x 8¼in) in size with butter.

Add the blackberries, sugar, chopped sage leaves, lemon zest and butter to a pan and heat until the sugar has dissolved and the berries are softened and syrupy but not mushy. If you are using frozen berries, this will take a little longer, about 6–8 minutes. Remove from the heat and leave to cool.

To make the sponge, melt the butter in the microwave or in a small pan and set aside.

In a large bowl, mix together the flour, caster sugar, baking powder, salt and ground almonds.

In a separate bowl, lightly whip the eggs, vanilla and cream, then pour into the dry ingredients. Pour in the melted butter and mix until the batter is smooth.

Spoon half of the batter into the baking dish, then pour the blackberry mixture on top. Spoon the rest of the batter on top – it won't completely cover all of the blackberries and that's fine. Sprinkle on the flaked almonds and demerara sugar. Bake for 30–35 minutes until golden and a skewer inserted into the middle of the batter comes out clean – it's fine if it has a little blackberry juice.

Serve warm with a splash of cream or a scoop of ice cream.

STONE FRUIT & BERRIES

peach & fennel cobbler

Nothing says summer like biting into a fat peach, its juices dribbling down your chin. Even better when it's cooked up in a cobbler, hot and bubbling underneath the buttery scone-like topping. The liquorice notes of the fennel bring a little complexity to the sweet peaches and add a little hint of savoury that I really appreciate in puddings. This is what I call a throw-together kind of dessert. The peaches don't need to be peeled or neatly sliced and the more scraggly the topping looks, the better.

Serves 6

For the peaches

600–650g (1lb 5oz–1lb 7oz) ripe peaches, washed and roughly chopped

60g (2¼oz/5 Tbsp) caster (granulated) sugar

1 tsp vanilla bean paste

1 tsp ground ginger

For the cobbler

1½ tsp fennel seeds

175g (6oz/1⅓ cups) plain (all-purpose) flour

30g (1oz/2½ Tbsp) caster (granulated) sugar

¼ tsp salt

1½ tsp baking powder

75g (2½oz/⅓ cup) cold unsalted butter, cubed

150ml (5fl oz/scant ⅔ cup) double (heavy) cream, plus extra for brushing

2 tsp demerara (turbinado) sugar

To serve

ice cream

Preheat the oven to 200°C (180°C fan/400°F/gas mark 6).

Add the peaches to a baking dish approximately 26 x 21cm (10¼ x 8¼in) in size. Mix in the sugar, vanilla and ginger, then set aside to macerate while you make the cobbler topping.

Coarsely grind the fennel seeds in a pestle and mortar and then set aside.

In a large bowl, mix together the flour, caster sugar, salt and baking powder. Add the cubed butter and use your fingertips to rub it into the flour until it resembles coarse breadcrumbs. Stir in most of the ground fennel, reserving a little to sprinkle on top of the cobbler later. Make a well in the middle of the mixture, pour in the cream and use a table knife to stir until the dough clumps together.

Make 6–8 rough balls of dough – you want them to be rough and scraggly, so don't overwork them. Place the balls on top of the peaches, leaving some space between them with the peaches poking through. Brush the tops with cream and sprinkle on some demerara sugar and the remaining ground fennel.

Bake for 45–50 minutes until the cobbler is golden and the peaches are bubbling underneath.

Leave to cool for 10 minutes before serving warm with ice cream.

plum & pistachio frangipane tart

Think of this as a deep-dish galette. It's not completely free-form, but baking it in a pan allows you to pack in more filling. A hearty layer of creamy pistachio frangipane holds the weight of ripe, juicy plums, all wrapped in a flaky pie crust. My favourite part of making this is layering the plums, each one placed intentionally, overlapping the next. There's something really beautiful about a tart or pie just before it goes into the oven, so take a moment to admire the gentle folds of pastry and jewels of demerara sugar.

Serves 10

For the pastry

250g (9oz/scant 2 cups) plain (all-purpose) flour, plus extra for dusting

1 Tbsp caster (granulated) sugar

½ tsp salt

200g (7oz/¾ cup plus 2 Tbsp) cold unsalted butter, cubed, plus extra for greasing

7–9 Tbsp ice-cold water

For the filling

400g (14oz) ripe plums

2 Tbsp caster (granulated) sugar

½ tsp ground ginger

1 Tbsp demerara (turbinado) sugar

For the frangipane

130g (4½oz) shelled pistachios

120g (4¼oz/½ cup) unsalted butter, softened

120g (4¼oz/scant ⅔ cup) caster (granulated) sugar

1 tsp vanilla bean paste

2 eggs, plus 1 for egg wash

75g (2½oz/¾ cup) ground almonds

To make the pastry, add the flour, sugar, salt and butter to a large bowl. Rub the butter into the flour with your fingertips to get a coarse mixture with some chunks of butter still visible. You don't want it to be fine and even. Add the water a tablespoon at a time and stir with a table knife until it begins to clump together. Turn the dough out onto a lightly floured surface and give it a very brief, gentle knead to bring it together. Pat the dough into a thick disc, wrap in plastic wrap and chill in the refrigerator for 1 hour.

Preheat the oven to 200°C (180°C fan/400°F/gas mark 6) and grease a loose-bottomed 20-cm (8-in) baking pan.

Once chilled, roll out the pastry to about 5cm (2in) larger than the size of the pan and press it into the pan, letting the extra pastry hang over the edges. Chill while you make the filling.

If your plums are on the small side, slice them into quarters, otherwise slice them into eighths. Add them to a bowl with the caster sugar and ground ginger, mix to coat and set aside.

To make the frangipane, pulse the pistachios in a food processor until fine or use a sharp knife to chop them as finely as you can. Cream the butter, sugar and vanilla together for 3–5 minutes until pale and creamy. Beat in the eggs, one at a time, beating well after each addition. Add the ground pistachios and almonds and stir in.

Spoon the frangipane into the chilled pastry case, smoothing the top. Discard any liquid from the plums and arrange them on top, starting from the outside and working your way in, and letting them overlap a little. Fold the excess pastry over the plums and brush with egg wash. Sprinkle on the demerara sugar.

Bake for 20 minutes, then reduce the oven to 180°C (160°C fan/ 350°F/gas mark 4) and bake for a further 35–40 minutes until the pastry is deep brown and a skewer inserted into the middle comes out mostly clean (a bit of plum juice is fine). Let cool in the pan for 20 minutes before removing from the pan to cool completely.

STONE FRUIT & BERRIES

cherry cardamom cream buns

This sort of bun goes by many different names depending on where you're from: a Cornish split, a Kitchener bun, or a Roman maritozzi, to name a few. Whatever you may call it, just know it's delicious. A pillowy soft, cardamom-scented dough, dusted in sugar and filled to near bursting with a cherry jam and velvety swirls of cream. An absolute delight.

Makes 6

8–10 green cardamom pods

140ml (4¾fl oz/½ cup) milk

3 Tbsp water

35g (2½ Tbsp) unsalted butter, softened

280g (10oz/2 cups) strong bread flour, plus extra for dusting (optional)

1½ tsp fast-action dried yeast

50g (1¾oz/¼ cup) caster (granulated) sugar

¼ tsp salt

1 egg, beaten

For the cherry jam

250g (9oz) fresh or frozen cherries

60g (2¼oz/5 Tbsp) caster (granulated) sugar

zest of 1 lemon

To coat

4 Tbsp caster (granulated) sugar

¼ tsp ground cardamom

25g (1½ Tbsp) unsalted butter

For the cream

400ml (14fl oz/1¾ cups) double (heavy) cream

1 tsp icing (confectioners') sugar

1 tsp vanilla bean paste

Remove the seeds from the cardamom pods and crush them roughly with a pestle and mortar. Add them to a small saucepan with the milk, water and butter. Heat gently until the butter melts and the milk is steaming. Cover and leave to cool.

In the bowl of a stand mixer fitted with a dough hook, combine the flour, yeast, sugar and salt. Make a well in the middle, then strain the cooled milk into the bowl, discarding the cardamom seeds. Pour in the beaten egg. Knead the dough on medium speed for 6–8 minutes until it starts to pull away from the sides of the bowl. If kneading by hand, lightly dust your work surface with flour and knead for 10–12 minutes until the dough is smooth and elastic. The dough will be sticky at first but try not to add too much extra flour. Place the dough in a lightly greased bowl, cover and leave to rise in a warm place for 1–2 hours, or until nearly doubled in size.

Meanwhile, make your cherry jam. If using fresh cherries, remove the stones and roughly chop them. Add to a pan with the sugar and lemon zest. Bring to the boil and cook for 6–8 minutes until softened and syrupy. If using frozen fruit, this will take a couple of minutes longer. Remove from the heat and cool completely.

Line two baking sheets with baking paper. Once the dough has risen, knock out the air and turn it out onto a clean surface. Divide into 6 balls, rolling each one as tightly as you can. Place on the baking sheets, leaving space between them. Cover lightly with plastic wrap and prove again for 30–45 minutes, or until risen and puffy. Preheat the oven to 190°C (170°C fan/375°F/gas mark 5). Bake the buns for 13–18 minutes until golden. Cool on a wire rack.

When ready to assemble, make the coating. Pour the sugar into a shallow dish and mix in the cardamom. Melt the butter. Slice the buns down the middle, nearly all the way through. Brush the tops with a little melted butter, then dip them in the cardamom sugar.

Whip the cream with the icing sugar and vanilla until you just have soft peaks. Spoon into a piping bag. Open up the buns and put a heaped teaspoon of the cherry jam inside each one. Pipe some cream on top and serve. These are best eaten on the same day.

cherry & coconut tahini cake

My earliest memories of coconut cakes are from school lunchtimes – generous wedges of very dry and heavy cake saved only by a deep pool of custard. It put me off anything with coconut for a long time. However, over the last few years I've been on a mission to change that. Here, the pops of sweet cherries and the glug of tahini help keep this cake soft and moist with a crumbly, coconutty texture. Add a little cherry glaze for a burst of colour and this cake is a real delight.

Serves 6–8

120g (4¼oz/½ cup) unsalted butter, softened, plus extra for greasing

150g (5½oz/¾ cup) light brown sugar

40g (1½oz/3 Tbsp) tahini

2 eggs

130g (4½oz/1 cup) plain (all-purpose) flour

50g (1¾oz/⅔ cup) desiccated (grated unsweetened) coconut

1½ tsp baking powder

¼ tsp ground cardamom

¼ tsp salt

90g (3¼oz) cherries, pitted and halved

1 tsp sesame seeds

For the glaze

40g (1½oz) cherries, pitted and halved

½ Tbsp lemon juice

100g (3½oz/scant ¾ cup) icing (confectioners') sugar

Preheat the oven to 180°C (160°C fan/350°F/gas mark 4). Grease and line a 15-cm (6-in) cake pan.

Using a stand mixer or electric whisk, cream the butter and sugar together for 4–5 minutes until pale and fluffy. Add the tahini and beat for another minute. Add the eggs, one at a time, beating well after each addition.

In a separate bowl, mix together the flour, coconut, baking powder, ground cardamom and salt. Pour the mixture into the butter mixture and mix on low speed until combined.

Spoon the batter into the prepared pan and add the cherries on top, along with the sesame seeds. Bake for 50–55 minutes, or until a skewer inserted into the middle of the cake comes out clean. Turn the cake out onto a wire rack and leave to cool.

To make the glaze, add the cherries and lemon juice to a small bowl and mash with a fork. Pass the mixture through a fine sieve (strainer), squeezing and pressing to get out as much juice as possible. Add the icing sugar to the juice and mix until you have a smooth, pourable consistency.

Once the cake has cooled, drizzle over the glaze.

nectarine, rosemary & ricotta focaccia

Focaccia is such a versatile and wonderful bread to know how to make. Once you've got a good base, it's easy to switch up the toppings depending on your mood or to reflect the season. I always slow down and take my time when it comes to dimpling the bread right before baking. That feeling of the soft, supple dough, liberally doused in olive oil, giving way underneath your fingertips is a little magical and gets me every time.

Serves 12

350ml (12fl oz/1½ cups) lukewarm water

7g (³⁄₁₆oz/2¼ tsp) fast-action dried yeast

½ tsp caster (granulated) sugar

450g (1lb/3¼ cups) strong bread flour

1 tsp fine sea salt

3 Tbsp olive oil, plus extra for greasing

For the topping

3 ripe nectarines

½ red onion

2 Tbsp olive oil

1 Tbsp water

3 sprigs of rosemary

100g (3½oz/scant ½ cup) ricotta

flaky sea salt

In a jug (pitcher), mix together the water, yeast and sugar, and stir. The yeast should get a little foamy on top.

In a separate bowl or in the bowl of a stand mixer fitted with a dough hook, mix together the flour and salt. Make a well in the middle and pour in the olive oil and yeasty water. Knead for 10–12 minutes (or 6–8 minutes in the stand mixer). If kneading by hand, the dough will be quite sticky. Turn it out of the bowl onto a work surface greased with olive oil to help you knead, adding more oil when needed instead of extra flour.

Place the dough in a well-greased bowl, cover and leave to prove in a warm place for 1½–2 hours until well risen and puffy. Alternatively, if making ahead of time, place the covered dough in the refrigerator overnight. Just let it come to room temperature the next day before continuing.

Add a tablespoon of olive oil to a 23 x 33-cm (9 x 13-in) baking pan, at least 5cm (2in) deep. Tip the dough into the pan and use your fingertips to gently spread it out to the corners of the pan. It's fine if it doesn't completely fill the whole pan now – it will spread as it bakes. Cover the pan and let the focaccia prove for another 45–60 minutes until risen and a little bubbly.

Preheat the oven to 200°C (180°C fan/400°F/gas mark 6).

For the topping, remove the stone from the nectarines and cut into eighths. Slice the onion into crescents. Mix the 2 tablespoons of olive oil with the tablespoon of water and pour this onto the surface of the dough. Use your fingertips to press into the dough, making lots of little indents. Pick the leaves of the rosemary and scatter them across the surface, pushing a few into the dough. Top with the nectarine segments, sliced onion and dollops of ricotta. Sprinkle the dough with some flaky sea salt.

Bake for 27–32 minutes until the dough is well risen and golden. Remove from the oven and cool for a few minutes before taking out of the pan and placing on a wire rack to cool completely.

blueberry & lemongrass pavlova

I couldn't imagine life without pavlova. As one of my most-loved desserts, it makes regular appearances all year round and I simply switch up the topping to make use of what's in season. This blueberry and lemongrass number has become a popular one, with its perfumed, citrussy aroma filling the kitchen as the compote bubbles away. The smell of sunshine. You can let the lemongrass sit in the blueberries overnight, if you prefer a more strongly fragranced flavour.

Makes 6

For the meringue

1 tsp lemon juice

145g (5¼oz) egg whites

275g (9¾oz/generous 1¼ cups) caster (superfine) sugar

1 Tbsp cornflour (cornstarch)

For the filling

3 sticks of lemongrass

300g (10½oz) blueberries (fresh or frozen)

50g (1¾oz/¼ cup) caster (granulated) sugar

3 Tbsp water

To finish

500ml (17fl oz/2 cups) double (heavy) cream

1 tsp vanilla bean paste

Preheat the oven to 120°C (100°C fan/250°F/gas mark ½). Line two baking sheets with baking paper.

Start by making the meringue. Wipe the bowl of a stand mixer or a large bowl with a paper towel soaked in the lemon juice. This helps to remove any traces of grease that may be in the bowl. Add the egg whites to the bowl and whisk on medium speed until thick and foamy with soft peaks. Increase the mixer to high speed and add the sugar, one heaped tablespoon at a time, whisking well after each addition. Once all the sugar has been added, continue whisking for another 2–3 minutes until the meringue is thick and glossy. Rub a little bit of the mixture between your fingertips – you shouldn't feel grains of sugar, but keep whipping if you do. Add the cornflour and whip briefly to combine.

Spoon the meringue into 6 mounds on the baking sheets. Use the back of a spoon or an offset spatula to smooth the edges and make a dip in the middle for where the filling will sit later. Bake the meringues for 35–40 minutes until they are firm to the touch and easily peel away from the paper. Leave them in the oven to cool completely for a few hours or overnight.

To make the filling, wash and remove any dried outer layers from the lemongrass and use the end of a rolling pin to bash and bruise the stalks and release some of the aromatic oils. Tie them together with a piece of clean string. This will help you fish it out later.

Add the lemongrass to a pan with the blueberries, sugar and water. Bring to the boil, then let simmer for 4–6 minutes until the blueberries have softened and are syrupy. Let the mixture cool completely with the lemongrass still inside. You can make this up to 2 days in advance and store in the refrigerator. Just remove the lemongrass when you're ready to assemble.

Just before serving, whip the cream and vanilla together until just before you get stiff peaks. I like to do this by hand as it's easy to overwhip with an electric whisk. Spoon the cream onto the meringue shells and top with blueberry filling. Serve immediately.

mango & hazelnut choux puffs

Describing food as cute has become quite a habit of mine, but I can't look at these little choux puffs and call them anything else. I make these on days when I want to feel a little fancy, but if you've never made choux pastry before, it's a lot more straightforward than you think. The extra shell that goes on them is called craquelin and this not only adds a crunchy texture but also helps the puffs to retain their shape when baking. Light as air and filled generously with mango, the colour of sunshine, sweet cream and roasted hazelnuts, it's incredibly easy to eat three or four of these in one sitting.

Makes 16–20

For the craquelin

75g (2½oz/⅓ cup) unsalted butter

100g (3½oz/½ cup) brown sugar

100g (3½oz/¾ cup) plain (all-purpose) flour

For the choux pastry

60ml (2fl oz/¼ cup) milk

60ml (2fl oz/¼ cup) water

50g (1¾oz/3½ Tbsp) unsalted butter

½ Tbsp caster (granulated) sugar

75g (2½oz/generous ½ cup) plain (all-purpose) flour

¼ tsp salt

2–3 eggs

For the filling

300g (10½oz) fresh ripe mango

½ Tbsp caster (granulated) sugar

juice of ½ lime

To make the craquelin, beat the butter and sugar together in a bowl for a few minutes until pale and creamy. Mix in the flour and stir until you have a thick, smooth dough. Roll the dough out between two sheets of baking paper to about 2–3mm (⅛in) thick. Slide the sheet of dough onto a baking sheet and place in the freezer for 15 minutes.

Preheat the oven to 200°C (180°C fan/400°F/gas mark 6). Line two baking sheets with baking paper.

To make the choux pastry, heat the milk, water, butter and sugar together in a small saucepan and bring to the boil. Tip in the flour and salt all at once and stir continuously with a wooden spoon until the dough comes together. Continue to stir and cook for 2–3 minutes until the dough comes away cleanly from the sides of the pan. Remove from the heat and transfer the dough to the bowl of a stand mixer (or a large bowl if using an electric whisk).

In a separate jug or cup, lightly beat the eggs together.

With the mixer on medium speed, beat the dough briefly to cool it down a bit. Pour in some of the beaten egg, a little at a time, letting it fully incorporate before adding more. The mixture will look lumpy at first but will come together. Continue until you have a consistency that is slightly thicker than dropping consistency – it should hold a 'V' shape when you lift a wooden spoon from the bowl. You may not need to use all of the egg.

Transfer the dough to a piping bag and snip off the end to create a hole about 2cm (¾in) wide. Pipe blobs of choux pastry onto the prepared baking sheets, leaving about 2.5cm (1in) of space between them.

To finish

350ml (12fl oz/1½ cups)
double (heavy) cream

½ Tbsp icing (confectioners')
sugar, plus extra for dusting

2 Tbsp Frangelico liqueur

50g (1¾oz/⅓ cup) roasted
hazelnuts, finely chopped

Take the chilled craquelin dough out of the freezer and use a round cutter to cut out discs that are the same width as your piped choux. Place a craquelin disc on top of each choux and bake for 25–35 minutes until the choux puffs are a deep golden brown.

Remove the puffs from the oven and pierce the bottom of each choux with a skewer or toothpick to let the steam escape. Place them back in the oven for 3 minutes to dry them out a little before letting them cool completely on a wire rack.

To make the filling, blitz the mango in a blender or food processor until smooth. Transfer to a small saucepan with the sugar and lime juice and bring to the boil. Reduce the heat and simmer for 5 minutes, stirring frequently so it doesn't catch. Pour into a bowl to cool.

Whip the cream, icing sugar and Frangelico to stiff peaks and transfer to a piping bag fitted with an open star nozzle.

Use a sharp serrated knife to cut off the top third of each choux puff. Spoon some mango filling inside the base of each and pipe a swirl of cream on top. Sprinkle on a few chopped hazelnuts before topping with the lid of the choux. Dust with icing sugar before serving. Once filled, these are best eaten on the same day.

STONE FRUIT & BERRIES

almond apricot loaf

I usually call this a tea cake, not because it has any connection to the traditional English fruit bun, but because it's one of my favourite cakes to have with a big fat mug of tea. Not too delicate or too sweet with chunks of almonds and dried apricots running through. I'm a big fan of using dried fruits, as they not only seem to last forever, but they're also an easy way to spruce up a really simple cake. Soaking the apricots in hot water first rehydrates them, making them a bit more plump and juicy. I've also used a longer, narrower loaf pan here purely because I love the way it looks, giving smaller, more chunky slices.

Serves 8

225g (8oz/1 cup) unsalted butter, softened, plus extra for greasing

150g (½oz) dried apricots, chopped into 1cm (½in) chunks

300g (10½oz/1½ cups) caster (granulated) sugar

2 Tbsp amaretto liqueur or ½ tsp almond extract

3 eggs

200g (7oz/1½ cups) plain (all-purpose) flour

40g (1½oz/scant ⅓ cup) ground almonds

2 tsp baking powder

¼ tsp salt

80g (2¾oz/scant ½ cup) plain yoghurt

100g (3½oz) whole almonds, roughly chopped

icing (confectioners') sugar, for dusting

Preheat the oven to 180°C (160°C fan/350°F/gas mark 4). Grease and line a 32 x 13-cm (12¾ x 5-in) loaf pan. Bring a kettle of water to the boil.

Put the dried apricots in a small bowl and pour over just enough boiling water to cover. Leave to soak for 20 minutes.

Beat the butter, sugar and amaretto or almond extract together for 4–6 minutes in a stand mixer or with an electric whisk until very pale and fluffy. Make sure to scrape down the sides of the bowl every so often. Add in the eggs, one at time, beating really well after each addition.

In a separate bowl, mix together the flour, ground almonds, baking powder and salt. Drain the apricots and toss them in the flour mixture. Pour half of this mixture into the butter mixture and mix on low speed until just combined. Stir in the yoghurt, followed by the rest of the flour mixture and the chopped almonds.

Pour the batter into the pan and bake for 50–60 minutes, or until a skewer inserted into the middle of the cake comes out clean. Let the cake cool completely before dusting with icing sugar to serve.

raspberry yoghurt honey cake

This cake has summer garden party written all over it. Summers in the UK are anything but predictable, so even if the heavens decide to open, this cake should still bring in a bit of sunshine – fresh and bright with a good tang from the yoghurt and pops of bright raspberries in both the sponge and filling. I like to use a really delicate and floral honey here to complement the summery vibes, but feel free to play around with your favourite varieties.

Serves 6–8

100ml (3½fl oz/scant ½ cup) sunflower or vegetable oil, plus extra for greasing

50g (1¾oz/3½ Tbsp) unsalted butter, melted

150g (5½oz/¾ cup) caster (granulated) sugar

1 tsp vanilla bean paste

3 eggs

120g (4¼oz/generous ½ cup) Greek yoghurt

50g (1¾oz/2½ Tbsp) honey

230g (8oz/1¾ cups) plain (all-purpose) flour

1½ tsp baking powder

¼ tsp salt

200g (7oz) raspberries, plus extra to decorate

icing (confectioners') sugar, for dusting

For the filling

200g (7oz/scant 1 cup) Greek yoghurt

150ml (5fl oz/scant ⅔ cup) double (heavy) cream

½ Tbsp honey, plus extra to decorate

Preheat the oven to 180°C (160°C fan/350°F/gas mark 4). Grease and line two 15-cm (6-in) cake pans.

In a large bowl, whisk the oil, butter, sugar and vanilla together. Beat in the eggs, followed by the yoghurt and honey, mixing until smooth. Add the flour, baking powder and salt to the mixture, stirring until smooth.

Divide the batter evenly between the cake pans. Add the raspberries on top of the batter, pushing a few in and leaving some on the surface. Bake for 35–40 minutes until golden and a skewer inserted into the middle of the cakes comes out clean. Let the cakes cool completely while you make the filling.

In a medium bowl, combine the yoghurt, cream and honey. Whip together for a minute or so until you have a smooth mixture.

Once the cakes have cooled, level off any domed tops with a sharp, serrated knife. Spoon the filling on one half of the cake and top with more raspberries and a drizzle of honey. Place the other cake on top, top-side down, and lightly dust with icing sugar before serving.

STONE FRUIT & BERRIES

roasted black pepper strawberries & set yoghurt

I won't let a strawberry season pass me by without sticking a tray of them in the oven to roast. It gives them such a concentrated strawberry flavour, with a pool of sweet, sticky juice that I'm always tempted to pour on everything. The set yoghurt is refreshingly light with a nice tang, the perfect canvas for this summery treat. My little spin on strawberries and cream. When you need a simple, light dessert with very little hands-on time, here's your answer.

Serves 4

2 platinum-grade gelatine sheets

350g (12oz/generous 1½ cups) Greek yoghurt

120ml (4fl oz/½ cup) double (heavy) cream

100ml (3½fl oz/scant ½ cup) whole (full-fat) milk

90g (3¼oz/scant ½ cup) caster (granulated) sugar

1 vanilla pod, split lengthways, or 1 tsp vanilla bean paste

For the roasted strawberries

400g (14oz) ripe strawberries

30g (1oz/2½ Tbsp) caster (granulated) sugar

1½ tsp freshly ground black pepper, plus extra to serve

4 fresh mint leaves

Soak the gelatine leaves in a small bowl of cold water and leave them to soften for 5 minutes.

Add the yoghurt to a medium bowl, give it a whisk to loosen and set aside.

In a small saucepan, gently heat the cream, milk, sugar and vanilla until the sugar has dissolved. Drain the water from the gelatine and squeeze out any excess water. Remove the cream from the heat and stir in the gelatine until that dissolves too. Pour the cream mixture through a sieve (strainer) into the bowl with the yoghurt. Stir thoroughly to combine.

Pour the yoghurt mixture into individual glasses or ramekins. Chill in the refrigerator for 2 hours, or until set.

To make the roasted strawberries, preheat the oven to 200°C (180°C fan/400°F/gas mark 6).

Cut the larger strawberries in half and keep the small ones whole. Add them to a large roasting dish and mix in the sugar, black pepper and mint leaves. Roast the strawberries for 15–20 minutes, turning once halfway through, until they are softened but not mushy. Remove the mint leaves and let the strawberries cool in the dish.

When ready to serve, spoon the strawberries and some of the roasting juices onto the yoghurt and add an extra pinch of freshly ground black pepper.

vegetables

It might seem strange to see a vegetable chapter in a baking book, but I hope you don't skip past the gems in the next few pages. Roasted, grated, fried or chopped, veg bring such a unique flavour and texture to breads and cakes that not many other ingredients can. From the pumpkin purée incorporated into scones to the fried plantain nestled into the delicate quiche filling, there's a hearty and earthy sweetness that just feels so homely and grounding.

I've really leaned into using root vegetables throughout this chapter, as their versatility partners so well with both sweet and savoury recipes. They are cosy and familiar. Preparing the vegetables, as repetitive as it can sometimes be, invites a slowness that some days require. Peeling ribbons of parsnips, scooping out the seeds of a squash, pulling back the thick skin of plantain are small but necessary steps that I like to be fully present for in anticipation of what's to come.

squash & nigella-seed soda bread

Some breads I love because they require your time and attention. They need your whole day, proving, resting, folding and shaping. There are days when I need that. But there are times when I want the taste and smell of fresh bread a bit sooner, and that's where soda bread comes in. If you panic at the thought of kneading, then this is the bread for you, as the less it's handled, the better. There's such a beauty in the ease with which this comes together with simple ingredients, providing you with good bread quickly, without compromising on flavour.

This is best eaten on the same day with butter, or it also makes the perfect bread to dip into a hearty soup.

**Makes 1 large loaf
or 2 smaller ones**

350g (12oz) butternut squash, peeled

2 Tbsp olive oil

1 tsp ground cumin

½ tsp paprika

½ tsp chilli flakes

2 tsp flaky sea salt

350ml (12fl oz/1½ cups) buttermilk

250g (9oz/scant 2 cups) plain (all-purpose) flour, plus extra for dusting

250g (9oz/scant 2 cups) wholemeal (wholewheat) flour

2 tsp nigella (black onion) seeds, plus extra to finish

1½ tsp bicarbonate of soda (baking soda)

Preheat the oven to 210°C (190°C fan/400°F/gas mark 6).

Chop the butternut squash into 2-cm (¾-in) chunks and place on a baking sheet. Drizzle with the olive oil and add the cumin, paprika, chilli flakes and 1 teaspoon of the salt. Toss with your hands to make sure the squash is evenly coated in the spices.

Roast the squash for 25–30 minutes, turning halfway, until cooked through. Place the squash into a jug or bowl and mash with a fork. Pour in the buttermilk and stir to combine.

In a large bowl, mix together the flours, nigella seeds, bicarbonate of soda and the remaining 1 teaspoon of salt. Pour in the buttermilk and squash mixture and stir with a table knife until you get a shaggy dough. Turn the dough out onto a lightly floured surface, give it just a couple of quick kneads to bring it together and shape into a mound (or two if making smaller loaves). You're not trying to smooth it out, so try not to overwork it.

Dust a baking sheet with flour or line with baking paper. Place the dough onto the sheet and use a sharp knife to make a deep cross on top, about 4cm (1½in) deep. Scatter a few more nigella seeds over the top and bake for 45–50 minutes until well risen and the base of the loaf sounds hollow when tapped. (If you're making two smaller loaves, bake for 25–30 minutes.) Transfer to a wire rack and leave to cool before slicing.

roasted carrot & harissa galette

It's the free-form, effortless nature of galettes that I find most attractive. Not constrained by the walls of a pie pan or the expectation of perfectly straight edges, it's a beautifully humble, rustic bake that looks a little different every time you make it. This savoury version with its crisp, flaky crust and colourful, spicy filling is light enough to take along for a picnic and filling enough for a weeknight dinner.

Serves 8–10

For the pastry

110g (3¾oz/generous ¾ cup) plain (all-purpose) flour, plus extra for dusting

110g (3¾oz/generous ¾ cup) wholemeal (wholewheat) flour

150g (5½oz/⅔ cup) cold unsalted butter, diced

½ tsp fine salt

100g (3½oz) mature Cheddar, grated

60–80ml (2–2½fl oz/4–5 Tbsp) ice-cold water

For the filling

450g (1lb) heritage (rainbow) carrots

2 Tbsp harissa paste

1 Tbsp honey

½ tsp flaky sea salt

2–3 sprigs of fresh thyme, plus extra to garnish

150g (5½oz/⅔ cup) mascarpone cheese

1 egg, beaten

Parmesan, for grating

To make the pastry, add the flours, butter and salt to a large bowl. Use your fingertips to rub the butter into the flour. You want quite a coarse mixture, so a few small chunks of butter are fine. Stir in the grated cheese. Make a well in the middle and add the ice-cold water a tablespoon at a time, using a table knife to stir until the dough comes together. You may not need to use all the water.

Turn the dough out onto a lightly floured work surface and knead gently and briefly to bring the dough together. Flatten the pastry to a thick disc, wrap it in plastic wrap and chill in the refrigerator for 1 hour.

Preheat the oven to 220°C (200°C fan/425°F/gas mark 7).

Peel the carrots and slice bigger ones lengthways into quarters and smaller ones in half. Toss them in a bowl with the harissa, honey and salt and give everything a good mix with your hands to make sure the carrots are all evenly coated.

Arrange the carrots evenly on a baking sheet, making sure they don't overlap (you may need to use two baking sheets). Roast the carrots for 25–30 minutes, turning halfway, until they're fork soft. Set aside to cool a little until you're ready to assemble.

Finely chop the fresh thyme and mix with the mascarpone.

Lightly dust the work surface with a little flour and roll out the pastry into a large circle about 35cm (14in) in diameter. Spread the mascarpone over the pastry, leaving a 3cm (1¼in) border around the edge. Arrange the carrots on top of the mascarpone – you can have them all facing the same direction and overlapping a little or just arranged randomly. Fold over the edges of the pastry to enclose and then brush with the beaten egg. Grate some Parmesan on the crust and bake for 40–45 minutes until the pastry is well browned and crisp.

Remove from the oven, grate a little more Parmesan over the top and add some extra thyme leaves before serving warm.

VEGETABLES

pumpkin spice coffee scones

The arrival of autumn is marked by many things, one of them being pumpkin-spiced everything. Over the years, I've come to embrace it and these scones are my contribution to the party. Scones should always be an easy, effortless bake, so I've used canned pumpkin purée to keep it simple, but feel free to make your own if you've got some leftover pumpkins to use up. If you make these with the coffee glaze, they're great to eat as is, but a dollop of clotted cream will always be welcome on a scone.

Makes 8

450g (1lb/scant 3½ cups) plain (all-purpose) flour, plus extra for dusting

1 tsp ground cinnamon

½ tsp ground ginger

½ tsp ground nutmeg

¼ tsp ground cloves

85g (3oz/scant ½ cup) caster (granulated) sugar

1 Tbsp baking powder

¼ tsp salt

180g (6¼oz/generous ¾ cup) cold unsalted butter, diced

100ml (3½fl oz/scant ½ cup) milk, plus extra for brushing

130g (4½oz/generous ½ cup) pumpkin purée

1 egg

For the coffee glaze

100g (3½oz/scant ¾ cup) icing (confectioners') sugar

1 tsp instant coffee dissolved in 2 Tbsp hot water

1 Tbsp milk

Preheat the oven to 200°C (180°C fan/400°F/gas mark 6). Line two baking sheets with baking paper.

In a large bowl, mix together the flour, spices, sugar, baking powder and salt. Add the cold butter and use your fingertips to rub it into the flour until it resembles fine breadcrumbs.

In a separate jug or bowl, whisk together the milk, pumpkin purée and egg. Make a well in the middle of the flour and pour in the liquids. Use a table knife to stir until it clumps together to form a dough.

Turn the dough out onto a very lightly floured surface and pat into a rectangle about 2.5cm (1in) thick. Cut the dough into 8 squares and place them on the baking sheets, leaving about 3cm (1¼in) between them. Brush the tops with a little milk.

Bake for 15–20 minutes, or until well risen and golden. Transfer to a wire rack and leave to cool while you make the glaze.

Mix the icing sugar, instant coffee mixture and milk in a small bowl until you have a smooth, pourable glaze. You can stir in a little more icing sugar if you find it's too thin.

Pour the glaze over the scones and let it set for a few minutes before eating.

rhubarb, ginger & white chocolate cake

I can't be the only one who often forgets rhubarb is a vegetable. When in season during winter in the UK, the bright-pink stalks of forced rhubarb have me like a kid in a candy shop. I simply cannot resist buying it, if only just to admire its unique hue. When I do get round to using it, this is one of the things I go for. A wonderfully soft afternoon tea cake, warm with ginger and chunks of white chocolate snuggled around all the rhubarb. It can also double up as a pudding if served slightly warm with custard. The perfect antidote to those dreary January days.

Serves 6–9

200g (7oz/¾ cup plus 2 Tbsp) unsalted butter, softened, plus extra for greasing

150g (5½oz) fresh rhubarb

180g (6¼oz/scant 1 cup) light brown sugar

3 eggs

225g (8oz/1¾ cups) plain (all-purpose) flour

2 tsp ground ginger

1½ tsp baking powder

½ tsp bicarbonate of soda (baking soda)

¼ tsp salt

80g (2¾oz/generous ⅓ cup) sour cream, at room temperature

75g (2½oz) white chocolate, roughly chopped

Preheat the oven to 180°C (160°C fan/350°F/gas mark 4). Grease and line a 20-cm (8-in) square cake pan, leaving an overhang of baking paper to help you lift the cake out later.

Wash and trim the ends of the rhubarb. Chop into 2-cm (¾-in) chunks and set aside.

Cream the butter and sugar together using a stand mixer or electric whisk for 4–5 minutes until very light and fluffy. Scrape down the sides of the bowl every so often. Add the eggs, one at a time, and beat for a minute after each addition.

In a separate bowl, mix together the flour, ginger, baking powder, bicarbonate of soda and salt. Pour half this mixture into the batter and stir until just combined. Mix in the sour cream followed by the rest of the flour mixture. Stir in the chopped white chocolate.

Pour the batter into the prepared pan, smoothing the top, and arrange the rhubarb on top of the batter. Bake for 50–55 minutes until a skewer inserted into the middle of the cake comes out clean. If the cake looks as though it's getting too dark before it's cooked, cover it loosely with a sheet of foil and continue to bake.

Leave to cool in the pan for 15 minutes, then turn out onto a wire rack and cool completely before slicing up.

VEGETABLES

spring onion & comté buns

Bread and cheese? Say no more. Spring onions take centre stage here in these soft, pillowy buns, and although I use quite a few, they're not at all harsh, but have a more mellow, sweet, onion flavour. There's a bit of Marmite in the cream cheese base. Admittedly, I'm not normally a fan, but for any Marmite-haters out there, trust me on this one – it works super well to up the umami flavour.

Makes 10

400g (14oz/scant 3 cups) strong bread flour, plus extra for dusting

10g (¼oz/3¼ tsp) fast-action dried yeast

1 Tbsp sugar

1 tsp salt

200ml (7fl oz/scant 1 cup) lukewarm milk

1 egg, beaten

50g (1¾oz/3½ Tbsp) unsalted butter, softened, plus extra for greasing

For the filling

120g (4¼oz/generous ½ cup) cream cheese

1 tsp Marmite (yeast extract)

90g (3¼oz) Comté cheese, grated

8 spring onions (scallions), finely sliced

Mix the flour, yeast, sugar and salt together in the bowl of a stand mixer fitted with a dough hook or in a large bowl. Make a well in the middle and pour in the milk and beaten egg. Knead on medium-low speed for 6–8 minutes, or for 10–12 minutes by hand. Let the dough rest, uncovered, for 10 minutes.

Add the butter to the dough and continue to knead for another 5 minutes until the butter is completely incorporated and the dough is smooth and shiny. If kneading by hand, it will take a little longer for the butter to incorporate, but persist! Place the dough in a greased bowl, cover and leave to prove in a warm place for 1–2 hours, or until doubled in size.

For the filling, mix the cream cheese and Marmite together and set aside.

Knock the air out of the dough and turn it out onto a lightly floured surface. Roll it out into a large rectangle, about 35 x 25cm (14 x 10in). Spread the cream cheese mixture evenly across the surface and then top with the grated Comté and chopped spring onions. Starting from a long edge, roll the dough up as tightly as you can. Tidy up the ends by trimming with a sharp knife, then cut the log into 10 equal pieces.

Generously grease 10 holes of a muffin pan with some butter and place a roll in each one. Cover with plastic wrap and leave to prove for 30–45 minutes until puffy.

Preheat the oven to 200°C (180°C fan/400°F/gas mark 6).

Bake the buns for 18–25 minutes until golden brown. Let them cool for few minutes before removing from the pan and allowing them to cool completely on a wire rack.

plantain & fennel quiche

My love for plantain is endless. It's a staple in our kitchen and as soon as the skin develops enough black spots to show its ripeness, it doesn't hang around very long. Soft and sweet, the fried plantains sit among the aniseed-scented fennel in the custardy filling, making an unexpected but delicious pairing. The recipe makes six individual quiches, but it will give you a few more if your cases are on the shallow side.

Makes 6

For the pastry

200g (7oz/1½ cups) plain (all-purpose) flour, plus extra for dusting

120g (4¼oz/½ cup) unsalted butter

½ tsp fine sea salt

1 egg yolk

2–4 Tbsp cold water

For the filling

2 eggs

275ml (9½fl oz/scant 1¼ cups) double (heavy) cream

1 large ripe plantain

1 red onion

1 fennel bulb

2 Tbsp olive oil

1 garlic clove, minced/grated

2 sprigs of fresh thyme, leaves picked, plus extra to garnish

50g (1¾oz) Gruyère cheese, grated

sea salt and freshly ground black pepper

Start by making the pastry. Pulse the flour, butter and salt in a food processor until fine. Alternatively, rub the butter into the flour with your fingertips if making by hand. Add the egg yolk and 2 tablespoons of the cold water. Pulse or stir until the pastry starts to clump together. Add more water, a tablespoon at a time, if the pastry is too dry.

Turn the dough out onto a clean surface and give it a couple of quick, light kneads to bring it together. Flatten it into a thick disc, wrap in plastic wrap and chill in the refrigerator for 1–2 hours, or until firm.

Once chilled, roll the dough out on a lightly floured surface to about 5mm (¼in) thick. Get six 10-cm (4-in) round tart pans ready – there's no need to grease them. Cut out 6 pastry circles slightly larger than your tart pans and press them into the pans, leaving a little pastry overhanging the sides. You may need to re-roll the pastry to get all 6 circles. Prick the bases with a fork, and line the cases with pieces of scrunched-up baking paper. Fill with baking beans or uncooked rice, then chill the pastry for 15 minutes.

Meanwhile, preheat the oven to 190°C (170°C fan/375°F/gas mark 5).

Bake the tart cases for 20 minutes before carefully removing the baking beans and paper. Place them back in the oven and bake for a further 7–10 minutes, or until the pastry is golden. Remove from the oven and set aside to cool.

Meanwhile, prepare the filling. Whisk together the eggs and cream along with a big pinch of salt. Set aside.

Peel and slice the plantain into rounds 5mm (¼in) thick. Finely chop the onion. Trim off the fennel fronds, cut the fennel bulb in half and then thinly slice.

Heat the olive oil in a frying pan over a medium heat, add the plantain and fry, turning a few times until golden brown. Remove from the pan and set aside. Using the same pan, fry the onions and fennel for 8–10 minutes until the fennel is soft and translucent. Stir in the grated garlic and thyme leaves and fry for another minute. Season with salt and pepper before removing from the heat.

When you're ready to assemble, sprinkle a little of the grated Gruyère on the base of the pastry cases. Split the fennel and onion mixture evenly among the tarts and top with a few slices of the fried plantain. Add a little more cheese on top, along with some more thyme. Pour the egg and cream mixture into the cases, filling to the top.

Bake the quiches for 18–22 minutes until the eggs are set with a little wobble in the middle. Remove from the oven and let cool for 20 minutes before serving a little warm.

parsnip, orange & ginger loaf

When it comes to vegetables in cakes, carrots tend to get all the love, but parsnips deserve just as much attention. Sweet and earthy with a subtle woody fragrance, this is a truly autumnal cake, with the grated parsnips keeping it perfectly moist. The parsnip crisps will make more than you need, but they make such a moreish snack I won't be offended nor surprised if none of them actually make it onto the cake.

Serves 8–10

For the parsnip crisps

1 parsnip

1 tsp olive oil

2 tsp maple syrup or honey

pinch of salt

For the cake

160ml (5¼fl oz/⅔ cup) sunflower or vegetable oil, plus extra for greasing

160g (5¾oz/¾ cup plus 1 Tbsp) light brown sugar

zest of 1 orange

2 eggs

200g (7oz) parsnips, grated

210g (7½oz/1½ cups) plain (all-purpose) flour

1½ tsp baking powder

½ tsp bicarbonate of soda (baking soda)

2 tsp ground ginger

¼ tsp ground cloves

60g (2¼oz) walnuts, roughly chopped, plus extra to decorate

For the glaze

90g (3¼oz/⅔ cup) icing (confectioners') sugar

juice of ½ orange

Preheat the oven to 180°C (160°C fan/350°F/gas mark 4). Line a baking sheet with baking paper and grease and line a 900-g (2-lb) loaf pan.

Start by making the parsnip crisps. Use a mandoline or potato peeler to thinly slice the parsnip. Place the peelings on the baking sheet and drizzle with the oil, maple syrup or honey and pinch of salt. Toss them with your hands to make sure all the pieces are coated and lay them out evenly so they don't overlap. Bake for 15–20 minutes, turning once halfway through. Keep a close eye on them, as they can catch quite easily. Remove from the oven and set aside to cool.

For the cake, mix together the oil, sugar and orange zest in a bowl. Beat in the eggs and stir until smooth, then carefully mix in the grated parsnips.

In a separate bowl, mix together the flour, baking powder, bicarbonate of soda, ground ginger and cloves. Add to the wet ingredients and mix gently until just combined. Now stir in the chopped walnuts.

Pour the batter into the loaf pan and bake for 45–50 minutes or until a skewer inserted into the middle of the cake comes out clean. Remove from the oven and leave to cool in the pan for 15 minutes before turning out onto a wire rack to cool completely.

To make the glaze, mix the icing sugar and orange juice in a small bowl until smooth. You want it to be a thick but pourable consistency. Add a little more icing sugar if it's too thin or a bit more orange juice if it's too thick.

Once the cake is completely cool, pour the glaze on top, letting it drip down the sides. Top with the parsnip crisps and extra chopped walnuts before serving.

sweet potato, chorizo & spinach turnovers

The sound of paper-thin pastry shards shattering under the weight of your teeth after the first bite of these turnovers will make you do a little happy dance. They're filled to the brim with roasted sweet potatoes, with nuggets of smoky, salty chorizo and pops of green spinach running throughout. Butternut squash would also work well here, as would a smoky veggie sausage for a meat-free option.

Makes 6

For the rough puff pastry

325g (11½oz/scant 2½ cups) plain (all-purpose) flour, plus extra for dusting

1 tsp paprika

250g (9oz/1 cup plus 2 Tbsp) cold unsalted butter, roughly chopped

1½ tsp salt

9–10 Tbsp ice-cold water

For the filling

550g (1lb 4oz) sweet potato, peeled and chopped into 1-cm (½-in) chunks

2 Tbsp olive oil

pinch of salt

150g (5½oz) chorizo, chopped into small chunks

1 red onion, finely chopped

1½ tsp fennel seeds, plus extra for sprinkling

¼ tsp chilli powder (optional)

100g (3½oz) baby spinach, washed

1 egg, beaten

To make the pastry, add the flour, paprika, butter and salt to a large bowl. Rub the butter into the flour, keeping the butter pieces about the size of a walnut. Add the ice-cold water, a tablespoon at a time, and stir with a table knife to bring the dough together in clumps – you may not need to use all of the water. Wrap the dough in plastic wrap and chill in the refrigerator for 20 minutes.

Turn the dough out onto a lightly floured surface and roll it into a large rectangle, about 3–4mm (⅛in) thick. Fold the top third of the dough down to the middle and then fold the bottom third on top of that (like folding a letter). Give the dough a quarter turn, roll it out to a large rectangle again and repeat the folding. Wrap in plastic wrap and chill until you're ready to assemble.

Preheat the oven to 200°C (180°C fan/400°F/gas mark 6).

Spread the sweet potato chunks in an even layer on a baking sheet, and drizzle with the olive oil and a little salt. Roast for 20–25 minutes or until cooked through. Set aside for now.

Fry the chorizo chunks in a frying pan over a medium-high heat until they start to release their own oil. Add the red onion, fennel seeds and chilli powder, if using. Fry for a few minutes until softened. Add the cooked sweet potato, followed by the spinach, and cook until the spinach wilts. Remove from the heat and set aside to cool completely.

Roll the chilled pastry out to a large rectangle, about 3–4mm (⅛in) thick. Trim all four edges to neaten them up before cutting it into six squares. Spoon a heaped tablespoon of the cooled filling in the middle of each square. Brush two adjacent edges with beaten egg and fold over to form a triangle, pressing down the edges to seal. Use a fork to go around the sealed edges, pressing it into the pastry. Place the turnovers on a large baking sheet, brush with egg wash and sprinkle some fennel seeds on top.

Bake for 25–30 minutes until the turnovers are well browned and the base is crisp. Let them cool completely before serving.

potato & cauliflower curry pie

This pie is based on a personal favourite: aloo gobi, a hearty potato and cauliflower curry. It's warm with chilli, spices, ginger and garlic, and makes a real cosy, comforting bake. Each slice is just a warm hug. The lattice crust, studded with nigella seeds, not only adds to the flavour but is visually impressive – you can only be proud when you take this out of the oven. The process of latticing a pie is so incredibly calming once you get the hang of it. The rhythm of weaving sheets of pastry over and under, over and under, helps me be still for a moment and focus on the task at hand. I've tried to explain the process as best I can, but if you're a more visual learner, there are countless videos online that you can refer to.

Serves 8–10

For the pastry

275g (9¾oz/2 cups) plain (all-purpose) flour, plus extra for dusting

200g (7oz/¾ cup plus 2 Tbsp) unsalted butter

3 tsp nigella (black onion) seeds

½ tsp salt

5–7 Tbsp ice-cold water

1 egg, beaten, for brushing

To make the pastry, add the flour, butter, nigella seeds and salt to a large bowl. Use your fingertips to rub the butter into the flour until you have a coarse mixture with small chunks of butter. Make a well in the middle and add the water, a tablespoon at a time, stirring with a table knife until the dough starts to clump together. Turn it out onto a lightly floured surface, pat it into a thick disc and cut it in half. Wrap each piece in plastic wrap and chill in the refrigerator for 1 hour, or until firm.

To make the filling, bring a large saucepan of salted water to the boil and cook the potatoes for 6–8 minutes, until they've softened a little but are still firm. Drain and set aside.

Heat 3 tablespoons of the oil in a large, deep frying pan and fry the cumin seeds for 1 minute until they start to sizzle and smell fragrant. Add the cauliflower and turmeric to the pan and cook for 4–6 minutes, stirring often, until the cauliflower begins to soften. Remove the cauliflower from the pan and set aside.

Add the remaining 1 tablespoon of oil to the pan and fry the onion for 5 minutes until softened. Stir in the garlic and ginger and fry for a minute before adding the garam masala and ground coriander. Cook the spices for a minute and then add the tomatoes, stirring regularly until they start to break down. Season with salt before tipping in the potatoes and cauliflower. Stir in the fresh coriander, pour in the water, cover the pan and let the mixture cook over a medium-low heat for 8–10 minutes. Remove the mixture from the pan and set aside to cool completely.

Get a 23-cm (9-in) pie pan ready. Lightly flour your work surface and roll out one half of the dough to a few centimetres larger than your pie pan. Line the pan with the pastry, pressing it firmly into the edges and leaving an overhang around the rim. Add the cooled filling, then chill the pie in the refrigerator while you start work on the lattice.

For the filling

400g (14oz) waxy potatoes, chopped into 2-cm (¾-in) chunks

4 Tbsp sunflower or vegetable oil

1 Tbsp cumin seeds

250g (9oz) cauliflower, cut into small florets

½ tsp ground turmeric

1 onion, finely chopped

4 garlic cloves, minced/grated

thumb-sized piece of fresh root ginger, minced/grated

2 tsp garam masala

2 tsp ground coriander

2 tomatoes, roughly chopped

handful of fresh coriander (cilantro), roughly chopped

3 Tbsp water

salt

Roll out the second half of dough to the same size as the first and use a knife to cut strips of pastry. It's up to you how wide you want them – I tend to go for 2.5cm (1in).

Take the pie out of the refrigerator and arrange half of the strips on top of the filling in parallel lines, leaving about 5mm–1cm (¼–½in) of space between them. Lift up alternate strips of pastry, pulling each one back halfway and letting it rest on itself.

Lay a strip of pastry down in the middle of the pie, perpendicular to the first set and lying on top of the strips of pastry that were not folded back. Pull down the alternating folded-back strips of pastry so that they sit on top of this new strip.

Next, fold back the strips of pastry that weren't pulled back the first time and lay down another strip of pastry next to the first perpendicular strip. Pull down the folded-back strips of pastry as before. Repeat this process until the pie is completely latticed. Take your time with these steps and feel free to start again if you get a little confused.

Trim the excess pastry around the rim and use a fork to press down and seal the edges. Chill the pie for a final 15 minutes before brushing with the beaten egg.

Meanwhile, preheat the oven to 200°C (180°C fan/400°F/gas mark 6).

Bake the pie for 45–55 minutes until well browned. Remove from the oven and let it cool for 20–30 minutes before slicing up ready to serve.

roasted veg dutch baby with scotch bonnet jam

A Dutch baby is a cross between a pancake and a Yorkshire pudding. The whole thing is as light as air; the crisp edges puff up dramatically in the oven while the base stays soft, creating the perfect edible bowl that gets filled with a heap of roasted veg. I tend to make this when I've got lots of odds and ends in the refrigerator that need using up. Drizzle with a little pesto or Scotch bonnet jam to finish for a fuss-free brunch.

The Scotch bonnet jam recipe is for all my friends who have asked me time and time again to make this jam and bottle it up for them. I first served it at a brunch a few years back and it was such a hit. It's got a deep and sweet tomato flavour, kicked up a notch with a fiery Scotch bonnet. Absolutely divine with fried plantains and eggs.

Serves 3–4 (and makes a medium jar of jam)

1 red (bell) pepper, roughly chopped

1 courgette (zucchini), sliced into 1-cm (½-in) discs

½ red onion, quartered

150g (5½oz) mushrooms (I use mini portobello or chestnut/cremini), thickly sliced

2 garlic cloves, unpeeled

2 Tbsp olive oil

1 tsp flaky sea salt

1 tsp za'atar

2 sprigs of fresh thyme

For the batter

3 eggs

75g (2½oz/½ cup plus 1 Tbsp) plain (all-purpose) flour

1 Tbsp cornflour (cornstarch)

½ tsp salt

180ml (6fl oz/¾ cup) milk

1½ Tbsp unsalted butter

40g (1½oz) Gruyère (or other hard) cheese, grated

To make the jam, heat the oil in a large, heavy-based saucepan over a medium heat. Fry the onion and pepper for 2–3 minutes until they start to soften. Add the garlic and cook for a further minute. Tip in the tomatoes, chilli, sugar, red wine vinegar, soy sauce and salt. Give it a good stir, then bring to the boil. Let the jam simmer over a medium heat for 15–25 minutes, stirring every so often. The jam is ready when it is thickened, shiny and reduced by nearly half.

You'll need one large jar or two smaller ones to store the jam. To sterilize them, wash the jars and lids in hot soapy water. While still wet, place them upside down in a preheated oven at 180°C (160°C fan/350°F/gas mark 4) for 15–20 minutes until completely dry. Pour the hot jam into the sterilized jars, cover with the lids and leave to cool. The jam will keep in the refrigerator for up to 3 weeks.

For the Dutch baby, preheat the oven to 200°C (180°C fan/400°F/gas mark 6).

Add the red pepper, courgette, onion, mushrooms and garlic cloves to a large baking pan in an even layer. Toss with the olive oil, salt, za'atar and leaves picked from the thyme until everything is evenly coated. Roast for 30–35 minutes until the veg is cooked through and starting to char a little on the edges.

For the Scotch bonnet jam

1 Tbsp olive oil

½ red onion, chopped into 1-cm (½-in) chunks

1 red (bell) pepper, chopped into 1-cm (½-in) chunks

2 garlic cloves, minced/grated

450g (1lb) tomatoes, roughly chopped

1 Scotch bonnet chilli, finely chopped

200g (7oz/1 cup) light brown sugar

65ml (2fl oz/¼ cup) red wine vinegar

1 Tbsp soy sauce

1 tsp fine sea salt

Meanwhile, prepare the batter. Add the eggs, flour, cornflour and salt to a large jug (pitcher) or bowl. Whisk together until smooth with no lumps. Pour in the milk, a little at a time, whisking well. Once all the milk has been added, cover the batter and set aside until the veg is cooked.

Remove the tray of veg from the oven. Squeeze the garlic out of their skins and stir the roasted garlic through the veg.

Heat a 23–25-cm (9–10-in) ovenproof frying pan or skillet on the hob. Add the butter, swirling it around the pan until it foams. Remove from the heat, pour in the batter and sprinkle half of the cheese on top. Add the veg to the batter, keeping it mostly in the middle. Top with the remaining cheese and bake in the oven for 25–28 minutes, or until well puffed up and browned.

The Dutch baby will deflate a little once it's out of the oven, so serve immediately, with the jam on the side.

VEGETABLES

best of beige

Beige food is undeniably comforting food. It's the double carbs, the chunky slice of cake drowned in custard, the hot sticky puddings, the caramels and the almost-too-flaky-to-eat-without-making-a-mess sausage rolls. It's what you crave on the days when you're feeling ill or low, or on the days you want a cosy evening in on the sofa. It's the food that makes you want to lick the bowl. Fewer things feel like a big old hug compared to the joyful, belly-warming shades of beige and brown food.

When writing and styling recipes, I'm always tempted to brighten everything up by adding splashes of colour to break up the beige hues and cut through what might be perceived as dull. But I've come to embrace and celebrate that this sort of food doesn't need any extra frills to look more appealing. Whether it's pound cake or brown-sugar custard and everything else in between, the recipes in this chapter are strong enough to stand on their own two feet. What makes them special is how they make you feel and how absolutely, wonderfully marvellous they taste. It's always a good day to bake something beige.

malted brown butter pound cake

Not many cakes are as comforting as a pound cake. It's simple in both name and appearance, but that's where its beauty lies. Heavy with butter, the dense crumb is at home when thickly sliced and served alongside a big mug of tea. The trick in getting the best texture and avoiding the dryness that is so often associated with pound cakes is to really, and I mean really, beat the butter and sugar for a lot longer than you may expect or be used to. You want it super-pale and fluffy, so get that electric whisk on high speed and scrape down the sides of the bowl often. This is one of those cakes that gets better with age, a perfect one to make ahead.

Serves 8

250g (9oz/1 cup plus 2 Tbsp) unsalted butter, softened, plus extra for greasing

250g (9oz/1¼ cups) caster (granulated) sugar

2 tsp vanilla extract

3 eggs, at room temperature

250g (9oz/scant 2 cups) plain (all-purpose) flour

2½ Tbsp malted milk powder (such as Horlicks)

1 tsp baking powder

½ tsp salt

120g (4¼oz/½ cup) sour cream, at room temperature

Start by browning the butter. Melt the butter in a medium saucepan, stirring occasionally. After 3–4 minutes, the butter will start to foam, but keep stirring. Once the butter starts smelling nutty and fragrant and has darkened in colour, remove from the heat and pour into a heatproof bowl along with all the brown bits at the bottom of the pan. Let it cool to room temperature before chilling in the refrigerator. We want it to be a soft, spreadable consistency, so keep an eye on it and give it a stir every so often. If it gets too firm, just let it sit out at room temperature for a bit.

Preheat the oven to 180°C (160°C fan/350°F/gas mark 4). Grease and line the base and sides of a 900-g (2-lb) loaf pan.

Once the butter has firmed up enough but is still soft, add it to the bowl of a stand mixer fitted with the beater attachment along with the sugar and vanilla. Beat on medium-high speed for 6–8 minutes, scraping down the beater and sides of the bowl every minute or so, until the butter is super-pale and fluffy. Add the eggs, one at a time, and beat for 2 minutes after each addition, again scraping down the sides and bottom of the bowl frequently.

In a separate bowl, mix together the flour, malted milk powder, baking powder and salt. Pour half of the mixture into the butter mixture and beat on low speed until just combined. Add the sour cream and mix on low speed until combined. Pour in the rest of the flour mixture and mix until fully incorporated.

Pour the batter into the prepared pan and bake for about 50–60 minutes until a skewer inserted into the middle of the cake comes out clean. If the cake is browning too quickly before it's cooked, place a sheet of foil on top and continue to bake.

Let the cake cool for 15 minutes in the pan before removing it to a wire rack to cool completely.

hazelnut anzac biscuits

My friends at Juliet's Quality Foods in Tooting make the best Anzacs. They were the first to introduce me to this classic Aussie treat and now I have to order one (or more) to take home whenever I visit. Chewy, buttery and laden with golden syrup, they make wonderful vessels for ice-cream sandwiches, are great dipped in chocolate, and are sturdy enough for dunking. In other words, they're just the perfect everyday biscuit.

Makes 12–16

65g (2¼oz/⅓ cup) blanched hazelnuts

80g (2¾oz/scant 1 cup) jumbo oats

190g (6¾oz/scant 1½ cups) plain (all-purpose) flour

90g (3¼oz/1¼ cups) desiccated (grated unsweetened) coconut

½ tsp salt

150g (5½oz/⅔ cup) unsalted butter

150g (5½oz/¾ cup) soft brown sugar

70g (2½oz/3½ Tbsp) golden syrup

1 tsp bicarbonate of soda (baking soda)

Preheat the oven to 180°C (160°C fan/350°F/gas mark 4). Line two baking sheets with baking paper.

Roughly chop the hazelnuts and add them to a large frying pan along with the oats. Toast the oats and nuts over a medium-high heat, turning and tossing frequently. Once they start to smell toasty and take on a bit of colour, remove from the heat and pour into a large bowl. Add the flour, coconut and salt to the bowl, give it a good mix and set aside.

In a medium saucepan, melt the butter, sugar and golden syrup together. Bring to a simmer, then tip in the bicarbonate of soda, stirring constantly to combine. Once the mixture begins to foam and thicken, remove from the heat and pour immediately into the dry ingredients. Stir thoroughly until the dry ingredients are evenly coated.

Use a small ice-cream scoop or a tablespoon to measure out 12 balls of dough and place them on the baking sheets, leaving about 2.5cm (1in) between them. Flatten the tops a little.

Bake for 12–16 minutes or until the edges are firm. The biscuits firm up as they cool, but if you prefer a crunchier biscuit, bake them for 2–3 minutes longer. Let them cool on a wire rack before eating.

BEST OF BEIGE

banana, tahini & rum cake

There's a different type of banana bread or cake for every mood. Sometimes you need a firmer, slightly dense loaf that can be toasted and doubled up as breakfast. Other times, you might lean towards something with a softer, more cakey crumb, perhaps studded with chocolate. This banana cake feels very grown up and is perfect for when you're feeling a little fancy. It's spiked with dark rum and a generous glug of tahini for a more savoury, nutty profile but is still just as easy to make as any other banana bread. All you need is a couple of bowls and a wooden spoon.

Serves 8–10

For the cake

2 eggs

100g (3½oz/½ cup) light brown sugar

100g (3½oz/½ cup) dark brown sugar

75g (2½oz/⅓ cup) tahini

300g (10½oz) bananas

3 Tbsp dark rum

150g (5½oz/1 cup plus 2 Tbsp) plain (all-purpose) flour

100g (3½oz/¾ cup) wholemeal (wholewheat) rye flour

2 tsp baking powder

¼ tsp bicarbonate of soda (baking soda)

½ tsp ground cinnamon

pinch of salt

walnuts, to decorate

For the glaze

60g (2½oz/scant ½ cup) icing (confectioners') sugar

½ Tbsp dark rum

½ tsp tahini

1 tsp vanilla bean paste

Preheat the oven to 180°C (160°C fan/350°F/gas mark 4). Grease and line the base of a 20-cm (8-in) springform or loose-bottomed cake pan.

In a large bowl, whisk the eggs and sugars together for a minute or so until combined and just a little bit paler. Mix in the tahini.

In a separate bowl, mash the bananas with the rum. Add the bananas to your egg mixture and stir to combine. Add both the flours, the baking powder, bicarbonate of soda, cinnamon and salt. Stir until just combined.

Pour the batter into the prepared cake pan and bake for about 40–45 minutes or until a skewer inserted into the middle of the cake comes out clean. Leave to cool a little in the pan while you make the glaze.

To make the glaze, mix together all of the glaze ingredients until smooth and you have a pourable consistency. If it is too thick, add a teaspoon of water at a time to loosen.

Pour the glaze over the warm cake and let it set for 10 minutes before turning the cake out onto a serving plate. Top with walnuts to decorate and let it cool completely before serving.

spiced lamb sausage rolls

Beige food doesn't get better than a good flaky sausage roll, and when still warm from the oven, they become a particular weakness of mine. These are inspired by my favourite North African merguez sausages, packed with lamb, cumin and spicy harissa. I've also added in some dried apricots for a little sweetness. Serve them with a cooling yoghurt dip on the side – just mix plain yoghurt with some chopped fresh mint and coriander (cilantro).

Makes 8–12

For the rough puff pastry

275g (9¾oz/2 cups) plain (all-purpose) flour, plus extra for dusting

225g (8oz/1 cup) cold unsalted butter, diced

½ tsp fine sea salt

7–8 Tbsp ice-cold water

For the filling

1 Tbsp olive oil

1 red onion, finely chopped

2 garlic cloves, minced/grated

1 tsp cumin seeds

1½ tsp fennel seeds

½ tsp smoked paprika

2 tsp ground coriander

1 Tbsp harissa paste

400g (14oz) minced (ground) lamb

50g (1¾oz) dried apricots, roughly chopped

50g (1¾oz/1 cup) fresh breadcrumbs

finely grated zest of 1 lemon

1 tsp fine sea salt

To finish

1 egg, beaten

2 tsp sesame seeds and nigella (black onion) seeds

To make the pastry, add the flour, butter and salt to a bowl. Use your fingertips to briefly rub the butter into the flour. The mixture should be quite coarse – you want some larger pieces of butter. Add the water a tablespoon at a time and mix with a table knife until you have a rough dough. You may not need all the water.

Turn the dough out onto a lightly floured surface and roll it into a large rectangle, about 1cm (½in) thick, with a short edge facing you. Fold the top third of the dough down to the middle then fold the bottom third on top of that (like folding a letter – if the pastry starts to get too warm or sticky, let it firm up in the refrigerator). Give the dough a quarter turn, roll it out to a large rectangle again and repeat the folding. Wrap in plastic wrap and chill for 1 hour.

Roll out the chilled pastry and fold as above one more time, then chill for another 30 minutes or until ready to use. Meanwhile, preheat the oven to 200°C (180°C fan/400°F/gas mark 6). Line a baking sheet with baking paper.

To make the filling, heat the olive oil in a large frying pan over a medium heat, add the onion and fry for a few minutes until softened. Add the garlic and spices and cook for another minute until the mixture is fragrant. Stir in the harissa, then remove from the heat and pour into a bowl. Add the lamb to the bowl along with the chopped apricots, breadcrumbs, lemon zest and salt. Use your hands to mix, making sure everything is well combined.

Lightly dust the work surface with flour and roll out the pastry to a large rectangle about 3mm (⅛in) thick. Cut this lengthways down the middle to give you two long rectangles. Place a layer of the filling mixture down the middle of each rectangle and brush one edge of each piece with beaten egg. Pull over the other side of pastry to encase the sausage, pressing to seal. Slice each rectangle into 6 sausage rolls (or 4 if you want bigger ones) and place them on the baking sheet. Chill in the refrigerator for 15 minutes to firm up.

Brush the rolls with egg wash and sprinkle on the seeds. Bake for 35–40 minutes until golden and the bottoms are cooked. Cool a little before eating.

just the crumble

There are two types of people when it comes to a fruit crumble. Those who believe it's all about the fruit and don't mind just a sprinkle of buttery topping, and then there's the camp who like to go very heavy on the crumble and easy on the filling. This recipe is for the latter group. I've ditched the fruit altogether to bring the best little nuggets of crunchy, oaty crumble that makes for the most moreish snack. Spoon it into a bowl of hot custard, sprinkle on ice cream or swirl it into your morning yoghurt... the possibilities are *nearly* endless. Double up the recipe if you want a bigger batch.

Serves 6–8

100g (3½oz/¾ cup) plain (all-purpose) flour

30g (1oz/⅓ cup) jumbo oats

2½ Tbsp caster (granulated) sugar

4 tsp light brown sugar

pinch of ground cinnamon (optional)

75g (2½oz/⅓ cup) cold salted butter, cubed

Preheat the oven to 180°C (160°C fan/350°F/gas mark 4).

Add all the dry ingredients to a bowl and mix to combine. Add the cold butter and rub it into the flour with your fingertips. Keep going until you get a rough, clumpy mixture. Chill the mixture in the refrigerator for 15 minutes.

Pour the mixture onto a baking sheet and bake for 15–20 minutes until golden, turning it once halfway through.

Remove from the oven and let it cool completely – it will firm up as it cools. Store in an airtight container for up to 1 week.

BEST OF BEIGE

brown sugar custard

How much custard is too much? I like most of my puddings absolutely drowning in the stuff, the more the merrier. A steaming bowl of creamy custard can really bring a pudding together and just warm up your belly. This brown sugar custard is such an easy twist on the classic and brings cosy butterscotch, caramel notes. It's delightful on its own, perfect with a crumble or poured over a slice of the Everyday Cake (page 119).

Serves 4–6

3 egg yolks

90g (3¼oz/scant ½ cup) light muscovado sugar

2 Tbsp cornflour (cornstarch)

pinch of salt

500ml (17fl oz/2 cups) milk

200ml (7fl oz/scant 1 cup) double (heavy) cream

1 vanilla pod or 1 tsp vanilla bean paste

Whisk the egg yolks, sugar, cornflour and salt together in a bowl until smooth, thick and a few shades paler.

In a medium saucepan, heat the milk, cream and vanilla. If using a vanilla pod, slice it down the middle, scrape out the seeds and add to the milk along with the pod. Heat the milk until steaming, just before the boil, then remove from the heat. Take out the vanilla pod, if using.

Add a big splash of the hot milk to the eggs, whisking well while you pour. Add the rest of the milk in three stages, whisking after each addition.

Pour the custard back into the pan and cook gently over a low heat for 6–8 minutes, stirring constantly. Once the custard has thickened, remove the heat and pour into a jug (pitcher) to serve.

If at any point you find your custard has scrambled a little, remove from the heat immediately and pour through a fine sieve (strainer) to catch any lumps.

cornflake caramel peanut bars

These are for the days when you want to bake without actually baking. We used to make cornflake 'cakes' all the time at school. Mixing up the cereal with melted chocolate and putting them in cute cupcake cases would always make you feel like a proper chef. These versions have had a little facelift and bring a good sweet and salty vibe with added crunch from the nuts. If you are making with kids, then you'll need to take control of the caramel steps, but they can do all the mixing!

Makes 8

170g (6oz/6¾ cups) cornflakes

100g (3½oz/¾ cup) salted roasted peanuts, roughly chopped

250g (9oz/1¼ cups) caster (granulated) sugar

60g (2½oz/¼ cup) unsalted butter, softened

180ml (6fl oz/¾ cup) double (heavy) cream

½ tsp flaky sea salt

100g (3½oz/scant ½ cup) peanut butter

Line a 20-cm (8-in) square cake pan with baking paper.

Mix the cornflakes and peanuts in a bowl and set aside.

Heat the sugar in a medium saucepan until it begins to melt. Swirl the pan every so often to help it melt evenly. Once the sugar starts to turn a deep amber colour, give it a stir with a spatula or wooden spoon to get rid of any lumps. Be very careful here as the sugar is extremely hot. Add the butter. The sugar will bubble up, but keep stirring until it calms down. Slowly pour in the double cream, stirring as you pour. The caramel will bubble up again, so be careful not to touch it. Let the caramel boil for 1 minute, then remove from the heat.

Stir the salt and peanut butter into the caramel until smooth. Pour the caramel into the cornflakes and mix until evenly coated.

Spoon the mixture into the prepared pan, pressing it firmly into all the corners. Let it firm up in the refrigerator for 1 hour before slicing into squares or bars.

BEST OF BEIGE

everyday cake

This is for the days when I fancy cake on a whim, which is quite often to be honest. It's the sort of cake you have on hand 'just in case' someone pops round. The kind of cake you slice thickly and have with a giant mug of tea on the sofa. This is a perfectly dense one-bowl cake that stays moist for days, thanks to the oil and yoghurt combination. The beauty in this cake lies in its flexibility and forgiving nature. Bake it in a round pan, swap out the vanilla for almond extract, grate in a little nutmeg, or use olive oil for something a little more fragrant. Eat it hot with custard or have it toasted with butter and a drizzle of honey. It may be called the everyday cake, but it is anything but mundane.

Serves 8

225g (8oz/1¾ cups) plain (all-purpose) flour

180g (6¼oz/scant 1 cup) caster (granulated) sugar

2 tsp baking powder

½ tsp salt

grated zest of ½ lemon

3 eggs, beaten

3 Tbsp vegetable oil

100g (3½oz/scant ½ cup) unsalted butter, melted

2 tsp vanilla extract or ¼ tsp almond extract

100g (3½oz/scant ½ cup) plain yoghurt or sour cream

icing (confectioners') sugar, for dusting (optional)

Preheat the oven to 180°C (160°C fan/350°F/gas mark 4). Grease and line a 900-g (2-lb) loaf pan.

In a large bowl, mix together the flour, sugar, baking powder and salt. Stir in the lemon zest. Make a well in the middle and pour in the beaten eggs, oil, melted butter and vanilla or almond extract. Mix gently until completely smooth and there are no streaks of flour. Stir in the yoghurt or sour cream.

Pour the batter into the prepared pan. Bake for 50–55 minutes until golden and a skewer inserted into the middle of the cake comes out clean.

Turn out onto a wire rack and leave to cool completely before dusting with icing sugar, if using, to serve.

peanut butter cookies

One of my favourite recipes that I developed over lockdown were these cookies. At a time when going to the supermarket felt like survival of the fittest and eggs were tricky to come by, these vegan cookies saved the day many, many times. I've tweaked them a little from the original to allow for a shorter chilling time but, as with most of the cookies in this book, they freeze really well, allowing you to bake a couple at a time when you fancy them.

Makes 12–14

100g (3½oz/½ cup) light brown sugar

100g (3½oz/½ cup) caster (granulated) sugar

100ml (3½fl oz/scant ½ cup) vegetable or sunflower oil

70ml (2¼fl oz/4½ Tbsp) water

2 tsp vanilla bean paste

75g (2½oz/5½ Tbsp) peanut butter (smooth or chunky)

240g (8½oz/1¾ cups) plain (all-purpose) flour

55g (2oz/generous ½ cup) rolled (old-fashioned) oats

1 tsp baking powder

½ tsp bicarbonate of soda (baking soda)

¼ tsp fine salt

200g (7oz) dark chocolate, roughly chopped

flaky sea salt, for sprinkling

Add both sugars to a large bowl and pour in the oil, water and vanilla, mixing well. Stir in the peanut butter until smooth. Add the flour, oats, baking powder, bicarbonate of soda and fine salt and stir until all the flour is incorporated. Mix in the chocolate, then cover the bowl with some plastic wrap and place in the refrigerator for 2–3 hours, or until well chilled.

Preheat the oven to 180°C (160°C fan/350°F/gas mark 4). Line two baking sheets with baking paper.

Scoop the dough into balls using an ice-cream scoop or your hands. (If you want to freeze some dough, just place the balls in a freezer bag and bake from frozen for a few minutes longer.)

Place the cookies on the baking sheets, leaving 3–5cm (1–2in) between them to allow for spreading. Sprinkle a little flaky sea salt on top of each one.

Bake for 10–13 minutes until the edges have set but the middles are still a little soft – they'll firm up as they cool.

malted milk crème brûlée

This is a deeply malty, creamy, custardy pudding protected by a smoky shard of caramelized sugar. A match made in heaven. Crème brûlée is one of those desserts that sounds super fancy, and before I'd ever made one I assumed it was quite complicated. But if you can make custard, you can make crème brûlée. I like to make it in one large dish and just let everyone dig in, but it also works in shallow ramekins.

Serves 4–6

150g (5½oz) egg yolks (from about 8 eggs)

60g (2¼oz/5 Tbsp) caster (granulated) sugar, plus 1–2 Tbsp to finish

2½ Tbsp malted milk powder (such as Horlicks)

400ml (14fl oz/1¾ cups) double (heavy) cream

150ml (5fl oz/scant ⅔ cup) whole (full-fat) milk

1 tsp vanilla bean paste

Preheat the oven to 160°C (140°C fan/325°F/gas mark 3). Boil the kettle.

Whisk the egg yolks, sugar and malted milk powder in a bowl until combined. Set aside.

Heat the cream, milk and vanilla in a small saucepan until just before the boil. Pour a quarter of the hot cream into the egg mixture and whisk to combine. Continue adding the cream, whisking gently as you pour.

Pour all of the mixture back into the saucepan over a low heat and let the custard cook and thicken a little, about 3–4 minutes. Keep stirring, especially around the edges of the pan. Remove from the heat and pour through a fine mesh sieve (strainer) into your baking dish or ramekins.

Place your dish/es into a deep roasting pan and pour enough hot water from the kettle to come halfway up the sides of the dish/es. Be careful not to get any water in the custard. Bake for 20–30 minutes until the edges look set but there is still a jelly-like wobble in the middle.

Remove the dish/es from the roasting pan and let cool to room temperature before chilling in the refrigerator for a few hours or overnight.

When you are ready to serve, sprinkle 1–2 tablespoons of sugar evenly across the surface of the custard. Use a blowtorch to caramelize the sugar, keeping the flame moving until the sugar turns a deep amber colour. You can add more sugar and go back with the blowtorch to any spots that aren't even. Let the sugar harden before cracking in.

sticky toffee treacle tart

I'll start by saying this is a very sweet dessert and so I have to be in a very specific mood for this. For me, it needs to be a cold, wintry evening, with the wind and rain howling outside and I'm all wrapped up and cosy on the sofa needing a warm hit of sticky sugar. This tart is a mash-up of two British classics, full to the brim with squidgy, caramelly dates and the signature breadcrumb texture of a treacle tart. Serve with a splash of cold cream or, if you really want to go for it with all guns blazing, you can add a little pour of the toffee sauce on page 127.

Serves 10–12

For the base

200g (7oz) digestive biscuits (graham crackers)

100g (3½oz/scant ½ cup) unsalted butter, melted

For the filling

150g (5½oz) Medjool dates, pitted and roughly chopped

75ml (2½fl oz/⅓ cup) boiling water

½ tsp bicarbonate of soda (baking soda)

140g (5oz/2½ cups) fresh breadcrumbs

1 tsp ground ginger

¼ tsp ground cloves

½ tsp flaky sea salt

30g (1oz/1½ Tbsp) treacle

280g (10oz/generous ¾ cup) golden syrup

40g (1½oz/3 Tbsp) unsalted butter

2 egg yolks

3 Tbsp double (heavy) cream, plus extra to serve

Preheat the oven to 200°C (180°C fan/400°F/gas mark 6).

First, make the base. Crush the biscuits in a food processor or put them in a food bag and bash with a rolling pin until fine. Tip the biscuits into a bowl and pour in the melted butter, stirring until everything is evenly coated.

Pour the mixture into a loose-bottomed 20-cm (8-in) cake pan. Use the back of a spoon to press the mixture firmly onto the base and up the sides of the pan.

Bake for 10 minutes, then remove from the oven to cool. Turn the oven down to 170°C (150°C fan/325°F/gas mark 3).

To make the filling, add the dates to a bowl and pour over the boiling water. Stir in the bicarbonate of soda and let the dates soak and soften for 10 minutes. Use a fork to mash them up as much as you can.

In large bowl, mix together the breadcrumbs, ginger, cloves and salt. Set aside.

In a medium saucepan, gently heat the treacle, golden syrup and butter until melted. Remove from the heat and stir in the dates. Pour the mixture into the breadcrumbs and stir until evenly coated. Add the egg yolks and cream and mix until fully combined.

Tip the mixture into the biscuit base and bake for 35–40 minutes or until the filling is firm to the touch.

Let it cool a little and serve warm with a splash of cold cream.

BEST OF BEIGE

irish cream toffee lamingtons

I'll be honest, assembling these little cubes of cake can be a bit of a messy job, so just embrace it. There'll be toffee sauce on your fingers and desiccated coconut all over the counter, but that's the best bit about making these lamingtons! There are days when letting go and making a mess does you good. I make these fairly big because why not, but feel free to opt for smaller pieces. It's also an easy recipe to cut in half for making a smaller tray – just bake in a 20-cm (8-in) square pan.

Makes 12–16

For the sponge

120g (4¼oz/½ cup) unsalted butter, plus extra for greasing

150ml (5fl oz/scant ⅔ cup) milk

4½ Tbsp Baileys Irish Cream liqueur

1 tsp vanilla extract

4 eggs

280g (10oz/scant 1½ cups) caster (granulated) sugar

250g (9oz/scant 2 cups) plain (all-purpose) flour

2 tsp baking powder

¼ tsp salt

For the toffee sauce

50g (1¾oz/3½ Tbsp) unsalted butter

90g (3¼oz/scant ½ cup) dark brown sugar

200ml (7fl oz/scant 1 cup) double (heavy) cream

2 Tbsp Baileys Irish Cream liqueur

big pinch of flaky sea salt

30g (1oz) dark chocolate, roughly chopped

To finish

250g (9oz/2⅔ cups) desiccated (grated unsweetened) coconut

First, make the sponge. Preheat the oven to 180°C (160°C fan/ 350°F/gas mark 4). Grease a 23 x 33-cm (9 x 13-in) cake pan and line with baking paper, leaving an overhang to help you lift the cake out later.

In a small saucepan, gently heat the butter, milk, Irish cream and vanilla until the butter has melted. Remove from the heat and set aside to cool.

In the bowl of a stand mixer or using an electric whisk, whip the eggs and sugar on high speed for 4–5 minutes until thick and pale and doubled in volume. With the mixer still running, pour in the cooled milk and whisk for another minute to combine. Tip in the flour, baking powder and salt and whisk again until you have a smooth, runny batter.

Pour the batter into the pan and bake for 30–35 minutes until golden and a skewer inserted into the middle of the cake comes out clean. Turn out onto a wire rack and leave to cool completely.

Meanwhile, make the toffee sauce. Add all the ingredients except the chocolate to a small saucepan and bring to a simmer, stirring every so often. Let the sauce bubble and cook for 2 minutes before removing from the heat and stirring in the chopped chocolate. Stir until the chocolate has melted. Pour the sauce into a shallow dish and let it cool to room temperature.

When you're ready to assemble, pour the desiccated coconut into a shallow dish. Cut the sponge into 12–16 even squares. Dip each piece into the toffee sauce, making sure to coat all sides. Let the excess drip off before coating each side in coconut. Place on a wire rack to set for 10–15 minutes before serving.

goose-fat potato focaccia

If I'm going to go for double carbs, then this is the recipe I choose again and again. Incorporating the liquid gold that is goose fat into the dough lends a richer, more luxurious flavour and fluffier crumb. It's the perfect vehicle for mopping up those last pools of gravy, or to make an epic Sunday-roast-leftover sandwich.

Serves 12

450g (1lb/3¼ cups) strong white bread flour

1 sachet (7g/³⁄₁₆oz/2¼ tsp) fast-action dried yeast

1 tsp caster (granulated) sugar

1 tsp salt

300ml (10½fl oz/generous 1¼ cups) lukewarm water

80ml (2½fl oz/⅓ cup) goose fat, plus extra for greasing

To finish

4–5 Tbsp goose fat

5–6 new potatoes, thinly sliced

small handful of rosemary sprigs, torn into small pieces

flaky sea salt

Place the flour, yeast, sugar and salt in a large bowl or the bowl of a stand mixer and toss together. Make a well in the middle and pour in the lukewarm water and goose fat. (If your goose fat is still solid at room temperature, gently warm it in a small saucepan until it melts.) Knead the dough in the stand mixer for 5–8 minutes or use your hands to mix and form a rough dough.

Turn the dough out onto a clean work surface lightly greased with a little goose fat. Knead the dough until it becomes smooth and supple – this could take up to 10 minutes. The dough will start out quite sticky, but try not to add extra flour. Add a little more fat if the dough sticks to the worktop too much. Once kneaded, place the dough into a lightly greased bowl, cover and leave to prove in a warm place for 1–2 hours, or until nearly doubled in size.

Preheat the oven to 220°C (200°C fan/425°F/gas mark 7).

Pour 2 tablespoons of goose fat into a rectangular baking pan, about 38 x 26cm (15 x 10½in), and spread it around the whole pan. Tip the dough into the pan and use your fingers to gently spread it out to all four corners. If the dough resists and pulls back, let it rest for 5 minutes and then spread it out again. Cover with plastic wrap and let it rise again in a warm place for 45–60 minutes until puffy.

Drizzle 2–3 more tablespoons of goose fat on top of the dough and use your fingertips to make deep dimples in the dough. Toss the potato slices in a bit of goose fat and then arrange them on top of the dough along with the rosemary. Sprinkle over a big pinch of flaky sea salt.

Bake for 25–30 minutes until the focaccia is a deep golden colour. Let it cool for a few minutes before slicing and serving warm.

spice cupboard

A well-stocked spice cupboard can make even the most mundane of foods infinitely more exciting. It's a wonder what a grind of peppercorns can do to a simple shortbread or how a few strands of saffron can transform a bread and butter pudding. It's this transformative nature that I'm so enthralled by – all those little jars you've got stacked up and labelled are small but mighty. It doesn't take much to create something new and unexpected with just a quick rummage in that spice drawer, and the smells produced by these bakes are just divine.

A pinch of chilli for heat, a sprinkle of cinnamon for a familiar fragrance or a grating of fresh nutmeg can perk up everything from cakes to breads and puddings, so once you're comfortable with these recipes, feel free to play around and experiment! If you're not too keen on cardamom, start with a smaller amount and adjust until you hit your sweet spot. If you can't live without a bit of heat, up the chilli in the cornbread. I want these recipes to become your own as much as they are mine.

SPICE CUPBOARD

pink peppercorn & ginger shortbread

I'm usually drawn to pink peppercorns because of that beautiful hot pink colour. I've found myself using them a lot more in my baking rather than cooking, as they bring such a sweet, fruity spiciness that isn't as brash as other peppers. The little nuggets of chewy, crystallized ginger also come with their own gentle heat that really warms up these butter-laden biscuits. I like these on the chunkier side, but you can slice them thinner and bake for a couple of minutes less for something more crisp.

Makes 16–20

2 tsp pink peppercorns

200g (7oz/¾ cup plus 2 Tbsp) salted butter, softened

100g (3½oz/½ cup) caster (granulated) sugar

300g (10½oz/2¼ cups) plain (all-purpose) flour

½ tsp ground ginger

40g (1½oz/3 Tbsp) crystallized ginger, finely chopped

3 Tbsp granulated sugar, for coating

1 egg white, for brushing

Grind your peppercorns until fine using a pestle and mortar.

Use a stand mixer or electric whisk to beat together the butter, sugar and ground peppercorns for 3–5 minutes on medium-high speed until pale and fluffy. Stop and scrape down the sides of the bowl every so often. Reduce the mixer speed to low and add the flour and ground ginger, followed by the crystallized ginger. Beat briefly until just combined – you don't want to overmix here as the shortbread will come out tough.

Turn the dough out onto a clean work surface and divide in half. Roll each half into a thick sausage, wrap in plastic wrap and chill in the refrigerator for at least 2 hours or until completely firm.

Preheat the oven to 180°C (160°C fan/350°F/gas mark 4) and line two baking sheets with baking paper.

Pour the granulated sugar into a large, shallow dish or onto a piece of baking paper. Unwrap each log of dough and brush the outside with the egg white, then roll each log in the sugar to coat. Use a sharp knife to slice the dough into rounds, about 1cm (½in) thick. Arrange them on the baking sheets, spacing them 2.5cm (1in) apart. You may need to bake them in batches.

Bake the cookies for 14–18 minutes until the edges just start to brown. Let them cool completely before eating.

honey-glazed cumin & coriander cornbread

I love the versatility of cornbread. It's perfectly at home thickly sliced with eggs for brunch or dunked in a big bowl of chilli, and simply toasted with plenty of salty butter is always a good idea. Here, it's gently spiced with some cumin and coriander before being smothered in a buttery honey glaze, speckled with seeds and chilli. I always have a little moment when I'm pouring the glaze on top, mesmerized by how it glistens and slowly seeps into the surface.

Serves 8

100g (3½oz/scant ½ cup) unsalted butter, plus extra for greasing

250ml (9fl oz/generous 1 cup) buttermilk

2 eggs

125g (4½oz/⅔ cup) fine cornmeal (polenta)

125g (4½oz/scant 1 cup) plain (all-purpose) flour

1½ tsp ground coriander

½ tsp ground cumin

2 Tbsp caster (granulated) sugar

1½ tsp baking powder

1½ tsp bicarbonate of soda (baking soda)

½ tsp salt

small handful of fresh coriander (cilantro), roughly chopped

For the glaze

1 Tbsp pumpkin seeds

1 Tbsp sunflower seeds

1½ tsp cumin seeds

25g (1½ Tbsp) unsalted butter

½ tsp chilli flakes

1 generous Tbsp honey

big pinch of flaky sea salt

Preheat the oven to 190°C (170°C fan/375°F/gas mark 5). Grease and line the base and sides of a 900-g (2-lb) loaf pan.

Melt the butter in the microwave or in a small saucepan and set aside to cool.

Whisk the buttermilk and eggs in a small jug (pitcher) and set aside.

In a large bowl, mix together all the dry ingredients. Make a well in the middle and pour in the buttermilk mixture, followed by the melted butter and chopped coriander. Stir gently until the mixture is fully combined and you have no streaks of flour.

Pour the batter into the prepared pan and bake for 30–35 minutes or until a skewer inserted into the middle comes out clean. Remove from the oven and leave the cornbread in the pan while you make the glaze.

For the glaze, toast all of the seeds in a dry frying pan over a medium heat for 1–2 minutes. Add the butter and chilli flakes, stirring and letting the butter melt and foam. Pour in the honey and let the glaze bubble for 1 minute, stirring so it doesn't burn. Mix in the salt, then remove from the heat and immediately pour the glaze over the warm cornbread.

Let it cool before removing from the pan and slicing to serve.

za'atar granola

Savoury granola might sound a little odd at first – we're so used to granola being reserved for our morning yoghurt pots. This version is heavy with fragrant za'atar, a Middle Eastern spice blend comprised of dried herbs (usually a mix of oregano and thyme), sumac and sesame seeds. I mostly use this granola for added texture and flavour to sprinkle on soups or to top garlicky yoghurt or a bowl of hummus. It also comes in handy when I'm in the mood for a more savoury snack. As with most granolas, this is super-flexible, so feel free to customize to your preference. Throw in some hazelnuts, up the chilli or mix up the seeds.

Serves 10

2½ Tbsp olive oil

1 Tbsp honey or maple syrup

125g (4½oz/1 cup) jumbo oats

2 Tbsp pumpkin seeds

1 Tbsp sunflower seeds

1 Tbsp sesame seeds

1½ tsp poppy seeds

2½ Tbsp za'atar

1 tsp ground coriander

¼ tsp chilli powder

½ tsp flaky sea salt

1 egg white

Preheat the oven to 170°C (150°C fan/325°F/gas mark 3).

In a small saucepan, gently heat the oil and honey or maple syrup until combined. Remove from the heat and set aside.

Add the oats, all the seeds and spices and the salt to a large bowl and give it a good mix. Pour in the oil and honey and stir the mixture, ensuring everything is well coated. Mix in the egg white and transfer the mixture to a large baking sheet, spreading it out to an even layer.

Bake for 35–40 minutes, turning the granola once halfway. Keep an eye on the edges, as they can easily catch.

Once baked, leave to cool completely. Store in an airtight container for up to 1 week.

cardamom, pear & pistachio cake

This is my ideal kind of afternoon cake – pleasing to look at, not too sweet, but fragrant with spice and packed with creamy pistachios. Cardamom is one of my favourite spices and it's taken a lot of restraint to not sneak it into more recipes. The light, citrussy notes really brighten up the pears but don't overwhelm. You can buy cardamom that's already ground, but I prefer to use the green pods and grind them by hand in a pestle and mortar to get the freshest flavour and a slightly coarser texture.

Serves 8–10

180g (6¼oz/generous ¾ cup) unsalted butter, melted, plus extra for greasing

120g (4¼oz/generous ¾ cup) pistachios, plus extra to decorate

seeds from 6 green cardamom pods

3 eggs

200g (7oz/1 cup) caster (granulated) sugar

2 tsp vanilla bean paste

180g (6¼oz/1⅓ cups) plain (all-purpose) flour

1½ tsp baking powder

¼ tsp salt

2 ripe pears

2 tsp demerara (turbinado) sugar

Preheat the oven to 180°C (160°C fan/350°F/gas mark 4). Grease and line a 20-cm (8-in) loose-bottomed cake pan.

Blitz the pistachios in a food processor until fine, or chop them up as finely as you can. Grind the cardamom seeds using a pestle and mortar and mix them with the pistachios. Set aside.

In a large bowl, whisk the eggs, caster sugar and vanilla for a minute until combined. Add the flour, baking powder, salt and finely ground cardamom and pistachio mixture and mix gently until you have a thick, smooth batter. Stir in the melted butter, then pour the batter into the cake pan and set aside.

Slice each pear in half, keeping the skins on, and remove the cores. Slice the pears about 5mm (¼in) thick and arrange them on top of the cake batter, letting them overlap. Sprinkle the demerara sugar on top.

Bake for 40–45 minutes or until a skewer inserted into the middle of the cake comes out clean.

Let the cake cool in the pan for 15 minutes before transferring to a wire rack to cool completely. Sprinkle on some extra ground pistachios before serving.

SPICE CUPBOARD

smoked paprika & halloumi flatbreads

Soft, buttery flatbreads, smoky with paprika and filled with salty halloumi. As breads go, these come together quite quickly, with a short proving time and just minutes in the pan. Eat these warm as soon as they're cooked with some of the garlicky tomatoes spooned on top. Most of the time, I intend on making these as a side dish or accompaniment to dinner, but more often than not I find myself just making a double batch and having them as the main event.

Makes 6

For the flatbreads

50g (1¾oz/3½ Tbsp) unsalted butter, plus extra for greasing

2 tsp smoked paprika

320g (11¼oz/scant 2½ cups) strong bread flour, plus extra for dusting

1 tsp caster (granulated) sugar

1 tsp fine sea salt

7g (³⁄₁₆oz/2¼ tsp) dried instant yeast

120g (4¼oz/generous ½ cup) plain yoghurt

120ml (4fl oz/½ cup) lukewarm water

120g (4¼oz) halloumi, grated

For the tomatoes

150g (5½oz) vine cherry tomatoes, roughly chopped

1 garlic clove, minced/grated

1 Tbsp olive oil

½ tsp flaky sea salt

handful of fresh oregano, finely chopped

Melt the butter in a small saucepan over a medium heat until foamy. Stir in the paprika and let it all bubble for a couple of seconds before removing from the heat and pouring into a bowl to cool.

In a separate bowl, mix together the flour and sugar. Add the salt and yeast to opposite sides of the bowl. Make a well in the middle and pour in the yoghurt and lukewarm water, then pour in the cooled paprika butter and stir until you have a rough dough.

Turn the dough out onto a lightly floured work surface and knead for 6–8 minutes until you have a smooth, soft dough. Place the dough in a lightly greased bowl, cover and leave to rise in a warm place for 40–60 minutes until puffy – it doesn't need to double in size.

Turn the dough out onto a clean work surface and divide into six equal portions. Use your fingertips to flatten each piece into a rough circle, about 10cm (4in) in diameter. Sprinkle some halloumi on top and fold the edges of the dough in to cover, pinching to seal. Turn the balls pinched-side down and use a rolling pin to roll them out to about 15cm (6in) in diameter.

Heat a non-stick frying pan over a high heat. Cook the flatbreads, one at time, for 2–3 minutes on each side. (If you're not serving them immediately, you can place them in a preheated oven to keep warm.)

To make the tomato salsa, mix the tomatoes in a bowl with the grated garlic, olive oil and the salt. Mix in the chopped oregano before serving with the flatbreads.

spiced bread & butter pudding with saffron & dates

Croissants are my bread of choice here, because the tops get unbelievably crisp, and in a pudding that is mostly quite soft, I always welcome a bit of crunch. The warming saffron custard that seeps into the bellies of the croissants is earthy and grassy, infused with ginger and cardamom to brighten it up. You could let the milk steep overnight if you'd prefer a stronger saffron flavour and swap the croissants for brioche or thick, white bread instead.

Serves 4–6

240ml (8fl oz/1 cup) milk

300ml (10½fl oz/generous 1¼ cups) double (heavy) cream

8–10 strands of saffron

30g (1oz) fresh root ginger, grated

6 cardamom pods, lightly crushed

2 eggs plus 1 egg yolk

70g (2½oz/generous ⅓ cup) caster (granulated) sugar

4 large croissants, slightly stale

50g (1¾oz) dates, roughly chopped

1 Tbsp demerara (turbinado) sugar

Pour the milk, cream, saffron, ginger and cardamom into a medium saucepan and heat gently until just before boiling. Remove from the heat, cover and let the milk steep and cool for at least 30 minutes.

Preheat the oven to 190°C (170°C fan/375°F/gas mark 5). Get out a baking dish approximately 26 x 21cm (10¼ x 8¼in) in size.

In a separate bowl, whisk the eggs, egg yolk and caster sugar together briefly until well mixed and smooth. Set aside.

Use a sieve (strainer) to strain the milk and pour it back into the saucepan. You can add a few strands of saffron back into the milk if you want a stronger flavour. Gently heat the milk and bring to a simmer, then remove from the heat and pour it into the egg mixture in three additions, whisking as you pour until all the milk is incorporated.

Slice the croissants in half horizontally and layer half of them in your baking dish. Scatter half of the dates on top. Pour just over half of the custard on top of the croissants and let it soak in for a few minutes before layering up with the remaining croissants and dates. Pour on the rest of the custard and sprinkle the demerara sugar on top.

Cover the dish with foil and bake for 20 minutes, then remove the foil and bake for a further 15–20 minutes until the top is crisp and the pudding has just a little wobble.

Let it cool and settle for 10 minutes before serving.

five spice & turmeric milk bread

The first thing you notice about these rolls is their magnificent colour. On a dreary day, I'll make a batch of these just to feel a little brighter and to bring some sunshine into the kitchen. The rolls are ridiculously soft and squidgy, thanks to the Japanese 'tangzhong' method, which involves making a paste of flour and water that gets mixed into the dough. Fragrant and fluffy, these are good warm from the oven with butter, or filled with some pork belly – my favourite way to eat them.

Makes 9 buns

For the paste

30g (1oz/3⅔ Tbsp) plain (all-purpose) flour

120ml (4fl oz/½ cup) water

For the bread

350g (12oz/2½ cups) strong white bread flour, plus extra for dusting

1 tsp ground turmeric

2 tsp Chinese five spice

1 sachet (7g/³⁄₁₆oz/2¼ tsp) fast-action dried yeast

1 Tbsp caster (granulated) sugar

1 tsp fine sea salt

160ml (5¼fl oz/⅔ cup) lukewarm milk

2 eggs: 1 whole; 1 beaten for egg wash

50g (1¾oz/3½ Tbsp) unsalted butter, melted, plus extra for greasing

Start by making the paste. Add the flour and water to a small saucepan and whisk until you have no lumps. Heat gently and stir continuously over a medium heat until the paste thickens to a glue-like consistency. Transfer the paste to a bowl and let it cool in the refrigerator.

To make the dough, mix together the bread flour, turmeric, five spice, yeast, sugar and salt in the bowl of a stand mixer fitted with a dough hook, or in a large bowl if kneading by hand. Make a well in the middle and pour in the milk, the whole egg, the melted butter and the cooled paste. Knead on low–medium speed for 8–10 minutes until smooth and elastic. If kneading by hand, this will take longer, about 12–16 minutes.

Place the dough in a lightly greased bowl, cover and leave to rise in a warm place for about 1–1½ hours, or until doubled in size.

Once risen, knock the air out of the dough and turn it out onto a lightly floured work surface. Divide the dough equally into 9 pieces and roll each one into a tight ball. Line a baking sheet with some baking paper and arrange the balls in three rows of three, leaving a gap of 1–2cm (½–¾in) between them. Cover with plastic wrap or a clean dish towel and let them prove for another 30–45 minutes until puffy and starting to touch one another.

Meanwhile, preheat the oven to 180°C (160°C fan/350°F/gas mark 4).

Brush the buns with the egg wash and bake for 18–22 minutes until golden and well risen. Let them cool before serving.

cinnamon & clove coffee biscuits

Elaborately decorated Christmas cookies are something I wish I had the skill and patience for, but the thought of trying to get them all perfectly uniform stresses me out. These are one of my go-to biscuits during the festive season, when I'm in the mood for sugar and spice and all things nice. Warm from the cinnamon and cloves with a little coffee for bitterness, these get decorated with a simple glaze. Feel free to opt for an even simpler look – a light dusting of icing sugar would be just as effective.

Makes 12–20

200g (7oz/1½ cups) plain (all-purpose) flour, plus extra for dusting

60g (2¼oz/scant ½ cup) icing (confectioners') sugar

½ tsp espresso powder

1½ tsp ground cinnamon

½ tsp ground cloves

½ tsp salt

120g (4¼oz/½ cup) cold unsalted butter, diced

2 Tbsp milk

For the glaze

75g (2½oz/generous ½ cup) icing (confectioners') sugar

water, as needed

Add the flour, icing sugar, espresso powder, cinnamon, cloves and salt to a food processor and pulse to combine. Add the butter and pulse until you have a mixture that looks like fine breadcrumbs. Alternatively, if making by hand, add the ingredients to a large bowl and rub the butter into the flour until the mixture is very fine. Stir in the milk and pulse until the mixture begins to clump or use your hands to start squeezing the mixture to form a dough.

Turn the dough out onto a very lightly floured surface and gently knead for a few seconds to bring it together. Flatten the dough into a disc, wrap it in plastic wrap and chill in the refrigerator for at least 30 minutes.

Meanwhile, preheat the oven to 180°C (160°C fan/350°F/gas mark 4). Line two baking sheets with baking paper.

Roll out the dough between two sheets of baking paper to 3–4mm (⅛in) thick. Use different sized cutters to cut out shapes and place them on the baking sheets, leaving space between them.

Bake for 15–18 minutes until the edges are firm. Let the biscuits cool completely on a wire rack.

To make the glaze, add the icing sugar to a bowl and add water, a tablespoon at a time, until you have a very thick, pipeable consistency. Pour the glaze into a piping bag, snip a tiny hole in the end and pipe around the edges of the biscuits. Alternatively, you could just dip the tops of the biscuits into the bowl of glaze. Let the glaze set for 10–15 minutes before eating.

vanilla-bean cake

Vanilla gets a bad rap for being boring and I don't think that's fair! As the second most-expensive spice in the world, it's usually hard at work behind the scenes, elevating and adding aroma to everything from brownies to cookies and custards. This cake is all about the vanilla, so now's the time to splash out on some good, fresh pods. Madagascan is probably the easiest to get hold of, but do try out Tahitian or Ugandan if you can get your hands on some.

Serves 12–16

For the cake

300g (10½oz/1⅓ cups) unsalted butter, softened, plus extra for greasing

1 vanilla pod

240ml (8fl oz/1 cup) milk

320g (11¼oz/generous 1½ cups) caster (granulated) sugar

4 eggs

420g (15oz/scant 3¼ cups) plain (all-purpose) flour

4 tsp baking powder

½ tsp fine sea salt

For the Swiss meringue buttercream

230g (8oz) egg whites

300g (10½oz/1½ cups) caster (superfine) sugar

450g (1lb/2 cups) unsalted butter, softened

1 vanilla pod

¼ tsp fine sea salt

Preheat the oven to 180°C (160°C fan/350°F/gas mark 4). Grease and line three 20-cm (8-in) cake pans.

Use a sharp knife to split the vanilla pod lengthways and scrape out the seeds. Add both the seeds and empty pod to a small saucepan with the milk and heat gently until hot but not boiling. Remove from the heat, cover and let the milk infuse and cool for about 20 minutes. Once cooled, remove the vanilla pod.

Using a stand mixer or electric whisk, beat the butter and sugar together for 4–6 minutes until very pale and fluffy, scraping down the sides of the bowl every so often. Add the eggs, one at time, beating well after each addition.

Mix the flour, baking powder and salt together in a separate bowl. Pour half of the flour into the butter mixture, mixing on low speed to combine. Pour in the milk and give it a mix before adding in the rest of the flour.

Pour the batter evenly into the prepared pans and bake for about 32–38 minutes until golden and a skewer inserted into the middle of the cakes comes out clean.

Let the cakes cool in the pans for 10 minutes before turning them out onto a wire rack to cool completely.

To make the Swiss meringue buttercream, add the egg whites and sugar to the bowl of a stand mixer or a large heatproof bowl. Make sure there are no traces of fat or grease in the bowl, as this will stop your meringue whipping up. Set the bowl over a pan of simmering water and whisk the egg whites as they heat. Rub a little bit of the mixture between your fingertips – it's ready when it's hot to the touch and you can't feel any grains of sugar.

Remove the bowl from the heat and start whisking on high speed until you have a thick, stiff, glossy meringue and the bowl is cool to the touch.

Add in all the butter at once and continue to beat on high speed. The meringue will deflate and may start to look a bit runny or split. Don't panic! Keep whipping and it'll come together. (If it's still really runny after 5 minutes of whipping, chill it in the refrigerator for 10 minutes and then continue to beat.) Once the buttercream is silky smooth, scrape out the seeds of the vanilla pod and add to the bowl along with the salt. Give it another quick whisk to combine.

When ready to assemble, level any uneven cakes with a sharp, serrated knife. Place one layer on a cake plate or stand and add a scoop of buttercream. Spread it out evenly with an offset spatula and repeat with the next layer. Add the last layer top-side down to get a nice flat top. Apply a thin layer of buttercream to the outside of the cake, smoothing it with a bench scraper or palette knife. (A turntable or lazy Susan comes in really handy here.) Chill the cake for 20 minutes.

Apply the remaining buttercream to the cake. Feel free to decorate as you wish here by piping on the top or just using a spatula to add some swoops and swirls.

SPICE CUPBOARD

nutmeg caramels

These buttery, soft caramels are warm with nutmeg, with a teeny bit of miso for some saltiness. They'll definitely stick to your teeth a little if you have too many, which is why I like to wrap them up, put them in a pretty box or tin and gift them to friends. No need to wait for any special occasion, these are perfect for sharing just because.

You'll need a sugar thermometer when making these to ensure they get to the right temperature.

Makes 20–25

250ml (9fl oz/generous 1 cup) double (heavy) cream

½ tsp fresh grated nutmeg

1 tsp white miso

50g (1¾oz/2½ Tbsp) golden syrup

125g (4½oz/scant ⅔ cup) caster (granulated) sugar

150g (5½oz/¾ cup) light muscovado sugar

55g (2oz/scant ¼ cup) unsalted butter

Grease a 20-cm (8-in) square cake pan and line with baking paper.

Add the cream, nutmeg, miso and syrup to a large saucepan. Heat gently, stirring until everything is dissolved. Add the sugars and butter and bring the mixture to the boil. Let it bubble and simmer for 8–12 minutes, giving it frequent stirs until it reaches 125°C (257°F).

Remove from the heat and pour the caramel carefully into the prepared pan. Leave to cool.

Once set, slice into small pieces with a sharp knife and wrap up in baking paper or waxed paper.

SPICE CUPBOARD

sumac crispbreads

Delightfully crunchy and fragrant, with deep-red flecks of sumac running throughout, these crispbreads are incredibly moreish, so I always make a double batch and keep them close by for snacking. If the thought of making bread intimidates you a little, these are a great introduction, coming together in under an hour. If you want them neater, slice into rectangles or squares before baking, but I love cracking them up into wonky shards straight out of the oven.

Serves 4–6

175g (6oz/1⅓ cups) plain (all-purpose) flour, plus extra for dusting

½ tsp fine sea salt

2 tsp sumac, plus extra for dusting

pinch of chilli powder

¼ tsp baking powder

grated zest of ½ lemon

100ml (3½fl oz/scant ½ cup) milk, at room temperature

1 Tbsp olive oil, plus extra for greasing and brushing

1 Tbsp sesame seeds

flaky sea salt

In a large bowl, sift together the flour, fine salt, sumac, chilli powder and baking powder. Stir in the lemon zest, then make a well in the middle and pour in the milk and olive oil. Stir together and turn the mixture out onto a lightly floured surface. Knead briefly for 3–5 minutes until the dough is smooth. Place in a lightly greased bowl and leave to rest for 20 minutes.

Meanwhile, preheat the oven to 200°C (180°C fan/400°F/gas mark 6).

Divide the dough in half, dust with a little flour and roll out each piece on a sheet of baking paper to make it easier to transfer to a baking sheet. Roll the dough as thinly as you can before brushing the surface with a little more olive oil. Sprinkle the sesame seeds and some more sumac and flaky sea salt on top before transferring the dough to a baking sheet.

Bake for 12–15 minutes until the crispbread turns an even brown colour. Remove from the oven and allow to cool for 5 minutes before breaking them up to serve.

chocolate

I've never been one to turn down chocolate. Unless it's in ice cream – strangely that's the only form in which I'd rather pass. Whether it's a little square of milk chocolate to get me through long stints at my desk, a slice of warm chocolate cake with cold cream after dinner on a Friday night or a chewy chocolate cookie accompanied by a giant tea in the afternoon, I don't need an excuse or occasion to bake up something chocolatey. Unlike some of the recipes in other chapters that might feel more appropriate during a particular time of year, chocolate is the powerhouse that just works all year round. It's familiar and comforting, can be dressed up or kept casual and is such a reliable and staple ingredient in my kitchen.

Some days, I need the full richness of chocolate, intense and dark. The Flourless Chocolate, Olive Oil & Almond Cake (page 162) is perfect for those times. And there are other days when I want to experience the lightness and playful subtlety that chocolate can have. Recipes like my Double Chocolate, Rosemary & Hazelnut Roll (page 172) fit that bill, with the chocolate playing a more supporting role against the fragrant filling.

So as you chop, melt, stir and pour the chocolate in these recipes, have fun and just don't forget to lick the spoon.

flourless chocolate, olive oil & almond cake

Flourless chocolate cakes can often lean into a deeply fudgy, almost sticky texture, but this version still retains a bit of a cakey crumb that stays eternally moist thanks to all the ground almonds. It makes for a good celebration cake or something to serve after a cosy dinner party when only chocolate on chocolate on chocolate will do. Serve with a good splash of cold cream.

Serves 12–16

For the cake

75g (2½oz) dark chocolate

250g (9oz/1¼ cups) caster (granulated) sugar

150ml (5fl oz/scant ⅔ cup) extra-virgin olive oil

3 eggs

175g (6oz/1¾ cups) ground almonds

90g (3¼oz/scant 1 cup) cocoa powder

½ tsp bicarbonate of soda (baking soda)

½ tsp salt

150ml (5fl oz/scant ⅔ cup) hot water

For the ganache

175g (6oz) dark chocolate, plus extra chocolate shavings to decorate

220ml (7½fl oz/scant 1 cup) double (heavy) cream

Start with the cake. Preheat the oven to 180°C (160°C fan/350°F/ gas mark 4). Grease and line a 20-cm (8-in) cake pan.

Melt the chocolate in short bursts in the microwave or in a bowl set over a pan of simmering water. Set aside to cool.

In a large bowl, whisk together the sugar and oil. Add the eggs and beat until smooth, then mix in the melted chocolate.

In a separate bowl, mix together the ground almonds, cocoa powder, bicarbonate of soda and salt. Stir this mixture into the wet ingredients until fully combined. Pour in the hot water and give it a good stir before pouring the batter into the cake pan.

Bake for 40–50 minutes until a skewer inserted into the middle of the cake comes out clean.

Let the cake cool completely in the pan and in the meantime make the ganache.

Finely chop the chocolate and place it in a bowl.

Heat the cream in a small saucepan until steaming, just before it comes to the boil. Pour the cream onto the chocolate and let it sit undisturbed for 30 seconds. Start stirring slowly from the middle, working your way outwards until you have a smooth ganache. If there are still a few unmelted lumps, place the bowl over a pan of simmering water and stir until everything is melted.

Place the cooled cake on a wire rack and set the rack over a baking sheet or a sheet of baking paper to catch the chocolate. Pour the ganache over the cake, letting it drip down the sides. Use a palette knife to help the ganache drip to any uncovered areas.

Leave the cake to set for 30 minutes before covering in some chocolate shavings.

sweet toast brownies

The sweet crunchy cubes of bread that nestle in this batter are incredibly moreish on their own, so do try a few before baking the brownies. I can sometimes be a bit of a purist when it comes to brownies, rarely incorporating extras like nuts or frosting. Most of the time, I just want unadulterated chocolate: rich, fudgy and smooth. But once in a while, when I'm feeling a little playful, this is what I'll go for. They bring such a good crunch and it's a fun way to use up leftover bread.

Serves 12

For the sweet croutons

60g (2½oz/¼ cup) unsalted butter, melted, plus extra for greasing

60g (2½oz) thick white bread

1 Tbsp olive oil

30g (1oz/2½ Tbsp) caster (granulated) sugar

20g (¾oz/¼ cup) milk powder

For the brownies

225g (8oz) dark chocolate

175g (6oz/¾ cup) unsalted butter

2 Tbsp cocoa powder

150g (5½oz/¾ cup) caster (granulated) sugar

150g (5½oz/¾ cup) light brown sugar

3 eggs

115g (4oz/¾ cup plus 2 Tbsp) plain (all-purpose) flour

½ tsp fine sea salt

100g (3½oz) milk chocolate, roughly chopped

flaky sea salt, for sprinkling

Preheat the oven to 180°C (160°C fan/350°F/gas mark 4). Grease and line a 20-cm (8-in) square cake pan.

First make the croutons. Cut the bread into small cubes and place them on a baking sheet. Drizzle them with the olive oil and toss to combine. Bake for 8–10 minutes or until firm.

Add the toasted bread to a bowl and mix in the caster sugar and milk powder. Pour in the melted butter and mix to evenly coat. Add the bread mix to a wide sauté pan set over a medium heat and stir frequently until the sugar melts and starts to caramelize with the milk powder. Remove from the heat and set aside.

To make the brownies, melt the chocolate, butter and cocoa powder in a bowl set over a pan of simmering water. Once melted, remove from the heat and set aside.

In a separate bowl, whisk together the sugars and eggs until smooth. Pour in the chocolate mixture and stir to combine. Mix in the flour and salt before adding the chopped chocolate and half of the croutons. Pour the batter in the prepared pan and top with the remaining croutons and a little sprinkle of flaky sea salt.

Bake for 40–45 minutes, or until the brownies are just set. Remove from the oven and leave to cool completely.

To get a super-clean cut, chill the brownies in the refrigerator for a couple of hours before slicing with a sharp knife.

CHOCOLATE

chocolate & date fruit loaf

Some of you might see fruit loaf and skip right past. Don't! I like to think of this as a fruit cake for people who don't like fruit cake. I originally developed this as a huge Christmas cake, but I've downsized it here for a more manageable loaf that you can have all year round, especially on those days when you crave a little taste of the festive season. Similar to a Christmas cake, this gets better with age, so it's good to make a day or two in advance to let all the flavours mingle.

Serves 10–12

200g (7oz) Medjool dates, pitted

100ml (3½fl oz/scant ½ cup) boiling water

½ tsp bicarbonate of soda (baking soda)

100g (3½oz/¾ cup) raisins

75g (3½oz/scant ¾ cup) sultanas (golden raisins)

50g (1¾oz/⅓ cup) dried cranberries

grated zest and juice of 1 orange

110g (3¾oz/generous ½ cup) dark muscovado sugar

90g (3¼oz/⅓ cup plus 1 Tbsp) unsalted butter

2 Tbsp brandy, plus extra for brushing (optional)

2 eggs

130g (4½oz/1 cup) plain (all-purpose) flour

50g (1¾oz/½ cup) ground almonds

2 Tbsp cocoa powder

1 tsp ground cinnamon

1 tsp ground ginger

¼ tsp ground cloves

½ tsp ground cardamom

½ tsp salt

100g (3½oz) dark chocolate, roughly chopped

50g (1¾oz/⅓ cup) whole blanched almonds

Preheat the oven to 160°C (140°C fan/325°F/gas mark 3). Grease and line a 33 x 13-cm (13 x 5-in) loaf pan.

Roughly chop the dates into small pieces and add them to a bowl with the boiling water and bicarbonate of soda. Give it a stir and leave for 10 minutes to soften.

Add all of the dried fruit, orange zest and juice, sugar and butter to a large saucepan. Heat gently until the butter and sugar melt, then let the mixture simmer for 3 minutes, stirring often. Remove from the heat, stir in the brandy (if using) and then mix in the softened dates, which should be quite mushy by now. Let the mixture cool for a few minutes before mixing in the eggs.

In a separate large bowl, mix together the flour, ground almonds, cocoa powder, spices and salt. Pour the fruit mixture into the bowl and stir until combined. Mix in the chopped chocolate and whole almonds before pouring the batter into the prepared pan.

Bake for 60–70 minutes or until a skewer inserted into the middle of the cake comes out clean.

When the cake is out of the oven, brush it generously with a few tablespoons of brandy (if using) and leave to cool completely. The cake will keep in an airtight container for up to 1 week. Wrap well in plastic wrap and a layer of foil to freeze.

miso & white chocolate cookies

Is there ever a day that can't be improved upon with a fresh baked cookie? The answer is no. Some days you need a thin, crisp, dunkable cookie and other days only a super-thick, weighty cookie like these guys will do. The miso brings a wonderful savoury umami hit that's contrasted with plenty of sweet, creamy white chocolate. You can either make ten very large and satisfying cookies, like I tend to, or if you want them to go further, you can make sixteen more regular-size cookies instead.

Makes 10 large or 16 small cookies

120g (4¼oz/½ cup) unsalted butter, softened

150g (5½oz/¾ cup) light brown sugar

75g (2½oz/6 Tbsp) caster (granulated) sugar

50g (1¾oz/3 heaped Tbsp) white miso

1 tsp vanilla bean paste

1 egg

290g (10¼oz/scant 2¼ cups) plain (all-purpose) flour

1½ tsp baking powder

½ tsp bicarbonate of soda (baking soda)

½ tsp salt

320g (11¼oz) white chocolate, roughly chopped

In a large bowl and using an electric mixer, cream together the butter, sugars, miso and vanilla on medium–high speed for about 6 minutes until really pale and creamy, scraping down the sides of the bowl halfway. Add the egg and beat for a further minute to combine.

In a separate bowl, sift together the flour, baking powder, bicarbonate of soda and salt. Add this to the butter mixture and mix on low speed until just combined. Stir in the chopped white chocolate.

Line two baking sheets with baking paper. Scoop the dough evenly onto the baking sheets and form into 10 large cookies or 16 smaller ones, leaving plenty of space between them for spreading. You don't need to roll them into a smooth ball; I quite like them with a bit of a craggy top. Cover with plastic wrap and chill in the refrigerator for at least 2 hours or overnight until firm.

Meanwhile, preheat the oven to 180°C (160°C fan/350°F/gas mark 4).

Bake for 15–18 minutes, or until the edges are set and the cookies are puffy.

Remove from the oven and let them cool before eating.

chocolate & fig bostock

Bostock is a recipe traditionally designed to use up leftover brioche, but as that never seems to be much of a problem in my house, I just whack the slices in the oven to dry out a bit before starting. If you want to spice up your weekend brunch offerings, then do give this a go. The honeyed sweetness of the figs against the chocolatey frangipane brings a real indulgent vibe to this easy bake. Add a dollop of crème fraîche to serve and you've got your day off to a pretty good start.

Makes 6

6 thick slices of brioche (stale or fresh)

3 ripe figs, quartered

60g (2¼oz/¾ cup) flaked (slivered) almonds

30g (1oz) chopped dark chocolate, to serve

drizzle of honey, to serve

crème fraîche, to serve

For the coffee syrup

70ml (2¼fl oz/4½ Tbsp) strong-brewed coffee

2 Tbsp caster (granulated) sugar

For the frangipane

120g (4¼oz/½ cup) salted butter, softened

120g (4¼oz/scant ⅔ cup) caster (granulated) sugar

¼ tsp almond extract

1 egg

120g (4¼oz/1 cup) ground almonds

1 Tbsp cocoa powder

1 Tbsp plain (all-purpose) flour

¼ tsp salt

Preheat the oven to 200°C (180°C fan/400°F/gas mark 6).

If you're not using stale bread, place the brioche slices on a lined baking sheet and bake for 5–6 minutes, turning them over halfway through. Remove from the oven and set aside on the baking sheet.

To make the coffee syrup, heat the coffee and sugar in a small saucepan, bring to the boil and let it simmer for 2 minutes. Remove from the heat and set aside.

For the frangipane, beat the butter, sugar and almond extract together with an electric whisk for 3–5 minutes until pale and fluffy. Add the egg and beat for another minute until combined. Mix in the ground almonds, cocoa powder, flour and salt to give you a thick paste.

When ready to assemble, brush the brioche slices generously with the coffee syrup. Spoon or pipe the frangipane on top of each slice and top each with two fig quarters and some flaked almonds.

Bake for 15–20 minutes until the frangipane is set.

Let them cool on a wire rack to stop the base going soft and serve with the chopped chocolate, a drizzle of honey and a dollop of crème fraîche.

double chocolate, rosemary & hazelnut roll

For me, the best part about making a Swiss roll or roulade is the process of rolling it up. The first time you give it a go it might feel a little scary but the trick is to be confident with it. Seeing a sponge become flexible enough to bend and furl, snuggling up to the soft filling as you carefully help it along is extremely satisfying. Don't be scared of any cracks either – embrace them. As long as you have fun rolling it up, there's nothing a good dusting of cocoa powder can't sort.

Serves 8

For the rosemary cream

300ml (10½fl oz/generous 1¼ cups) double (heavy) cream

2 large sprigs of rosemary

60g (2¼oz) white chocolate, finely chopped

For the sponge

90g (3¼oz/⅔ cup) plain (all-purpose) flour

20g (¾oz/3 heaped Tbsp) cocoa powder, plus extra for dusting

½ tsp baking powder

4 eggs

100g (3½oz/½ cup) caster (granulated) sugar

finely grated zest of 1 orange

2 Tbsp chopped roasted hazelnuts

Start with the rosemary cream, as it needs time to chill. Heat the double cream with the rosemary in a small saucepan until steaming, just before the boil. Remove from the heat, cover and leave to steep for 15 minutes.

Add the chopped white chocolate to a heatproof bowl.

Remove the rosemary from the pan and gently reheat the cream until hot but not boiling. Pour the cream over the chocolate and stir gently until smooth. Cover and chill in the refrigerator for 2 hours, or until completely cold.

Preheat the oven to 180°C (160°C fan/350°F/gas mark 4). Line a 23 x 33-cm (9 x 13-in) Swiss roll (jelly roll) pan or baking sheet at least 1cm (½in) deep.

Sift together the flour, cocoa powder and baking powder and set aside.

Using an electric whisk or stand mixer, beat together the eggs, sugar and orange zest on high speed for 3–5 minutes until thick, pale and nearly tripled in volume. You want the eggs to get to ribbon stage – when you lift the beaters from the mixer, the eggs should fall back in thick trails and stay on the surface for a few moments before disappearing. Sift in the flour mixture in three batches. Gently fold after each addition, being really careful not to knock out too much air. Make sure you're getting right down to the bottom of the bowl where pockets of flour may be hiding.

Once all the flour has been incorporated, pour the batter into the pan, again being careful not to knock out more air. Tilt the pan so the batter fills all the corners. Bake for 12–15 minutes until the cake feels springy to the touch.

Remove from the oven and let it cool for a minute. Place a sheet of baking paper that's a little larger than your pan on your work surface. Dust generously with cocoa powder and then invert the sponge onto the paper. Peel off the baking paper that is now on top and, starting from a short end, slowly and tightly roll up the cake (with the bottom piece of baking paper rolled inside with it). Place the roll seam-side down and leave to cool completely.

Take the rosemary cream from the refrigerator and whisk until it thickens to stiff peaks.

Once cooled, carefully unroll the sponge. Don't panic if you have any cracks! Spread the cream evenly onto the cake and sprinkle on the chopped hazelnuts. Re-roll the sponge in the same direction as before and place in the refrigerator to firm up.

When ready to serve, slice off each end to show the neat swirl and dust with a little more cocoa powder.

CHOCOLATE

store-cupboard cake

I came up with this during the very first lockdown of 2020, which now feels like a lifetime ago. It relies on using ingredients that you're already pretty likely to have in the kitchen, meaning you can whip this up anytime with minimal effort whenever the chocolate craving hits. It doesn't need any eggs or dairy either, so no need to pop out to get those. If there's anyone out there convinced that they can't bake, this is the perfect recipe to start with.

Serves 8–10

For the cake

120ml (4fl oz/½ cup) any neutral oil, plus extra for greasing

190g (6¾oz/scant 1½ cups) plain (all-purpose) flour

200g (7oz/1 cup) caster (granulated) sugar

30g (1oz/scant ⅓ cup) cocoa powder

1 tsp baking powder

1½ tsp bicarbonate of soda (baking soda)

¼ tsp salt

1 Tbsp white wine vinegar

½ tsp espresso powder or instant coffee (optional)

240ml (8fl oz/1 cup) hot water

Optional store-cupboard extras

jam, peanut butter, chocolate chunks, chopped dried fruit or chopped nuts

icing (confectioners') sugar, for dusting

Preheat the oven to 180°C (160°C fan/350°F/gas mark 4). Grease and line a 23-cm (9-in) cake pan.

In a large bowl, mix together the flour, sugar, cocoa powder, baking powder, bicarbonate of soda and salt. Make a well in the middle and pour in the oil and white wine vinegar. Give it a quick stir – it'll be quite thick at this point.

Dissolve the coffee in the hot water and pour half of it into the bowl. Mix until combined before adding the rest of the water and stirring until smooth.

Pour the batter into the cake pan and throw in any optional extras like a swirl of jam or peanut butter or a sprinkle of dried fruit or chopped nuts.

Bake for 30–35 minutes, or until a skewer inserted into the middle of the cake comes out clean.

Let the cake cool in the pan for 10 minutes before turning out onto a wire rack to cool completely. Dust with icing sugar, if using, before serving.

coconut, white chocolate & cardamom rice pudding

Some may say rice pudding is making a comeback, but did it ever really go anywhere? The rice pudding I make now is a vast improvement from what we got served for school dinners and still remains one of my favourite comfort puddings. It's a dessert that's fairly simple to make, but requires your full attention, as it needs to be frequently stirred. So, this is for the days where I'm drawn to a recipe that requires me to be present, to be still, and to use my time stirring as a welcome moment of calm.

Serves 4

30g (1oz/6 Tbsp) desiccated (grated unsweetened) coconut

100g (3½oz/½ cup) pudding rice

40g (1½oz/3 Tbsp) unsalted butter

seeds from 5 cardamom pods, crushed

40g (1½oz/3¼ Tbsp) caster (granulated) sugar

2 x 400-g (14-oz) cans full-fat coconut milk

300ml (10½fl oz/generous 1¼ cups) milk

1 tsp vanilla bean paste

60g (2¼oz) white chocolate, roughly chopped

In a large deep saucepan, toast the desiccated coconut over a medium heat, stirring frequently until it starts to brown. Pour the coconut into a bowl and set aside to serve.

To the same saucepan, add the rice, butter and cardamom. Toast the rice in the butter, stirring frequently until the butter is just starting to brown and the rice is nicely coated. Stir in the sugar, then add the coconut milk, milk and vanilla bean paste. Bring to a simmer, then let the rice cook for 45–50 minutes until soft. You'll need to stir frequently so it doesn't stick to the bottom of the pan. If the rice looks too thick at any point, just add another splash of milk.

Once the rice is cooked, stir in the white chocolate. Serve with the toasted coconut.

Store in an airtight container in the refrigerator for up to 3 days. To reheat, add a splash of milk and heat gently in a pan.

chocolate, tahini & marmalade biscuits

You could say that these are a cross between a bourbon biscuit and a custard cream... kind of. But just a little fancier? I love sandwiched biscuits because it feels like a 'two-for-the-price-of-one' sort of deal and I'm not one to pass on a good bargain. Two crisp chocolate biscuits, a good spread of custardy tahini buttercream and a little bit of marmalade for some sharpness – all that's left to do is put the kettle on.

Makes about 18 sandwiched biscuits

150g (5½oz/⅔ cup) unsalted butter, softened

80g (2¾oz/generous ⅓ cup) caster (granulated) sugar

20g (¾oz/1 Tbsp plus 2 tsp) dark brown sugar

1 egg

250g (9oz/scant 2 cups) plain (all-purpose) flour

75g (2½oz/¾ cup) cocoa powder

1½ tsp cornflour (cornstarch)

½ tsp baking powder

¼ tsp salt

3 Tbsp marmalade

For the tahini buttercream

150g (5½oz/⅔ cup) unsalted butter

200g (7oz/scant 1½ cups) icing (confectioners') sugar

2 Tbsp custard powder (instant vanilla pudding mix)

1 tsp vanilla bean paste

60g (2¼oz/scant ⅓ cup) tahini

Preheat the oven to 180°C (160°C fan/350°F/gas mark 4). Line two baking sheets with baking paper.

To make the biscuits, cream the butter and sugars together with an electric whisk for 2–3 minutes until smooth and creamy. Beat in the egg.

In a separate bowl, mix together the flour, cocoa powder, cornflour, baking powder and salt. Pour this into the butter mixture and mix on low speed until just combined.

Wrap the dough in plastic wrap and chill in the refrigerator for 30–60 minutes, or until firm.

Once chilled, roll the dough out between two sheets of baking paper into a 32-cm (12¾-in) square. Use a sharp knife to cut the dough into equal-sized rectangles. The size of these is up to you – you can go as big or small as you fancy. Arrange the biscuits on the baking sheets, leaving a small gap between them. Use a skewer to prick six holes on top of each biscuit (three rows of two).

Bake the biscuits for 12–15 minutes until the edges are firm to the touch. Leave to cool completely.

To make the buttercream, beat the butter in a bowl for 2 minutes until creamy. Add the icing sugar, custard powder and vanilla bean paste and beat for 4–6 minutes until very pale and fluffy. Add the tahini and beat for another minute.

When you're ready to assemble, spoon or pipe the buttercream onto half of the biscuits and spread a little marmalade on the other halves. Sandwich the biscuits together and serve.

warm dulce de leche marble cake

When a cake comes out of the oven, there are times when it takes absolutely everything within you to leave it alone to cool completely as so gently instructed. This little guy is an exception. You need to eat this warm, hunched over the kitchen counter, while the little rivers of caramel and pools of chocolate are still gooey. It's the perfect size for two and can be in the oven in less than 10 minutes, making it my ideal week-night dessert. So grab a friend, a couple of spoons and maybe a scoop of ice cream, because why not?

Serves 2

50g (1¾oz/3½ Tbsp) unsalted butter, plus extra for greasing

50g (1¾oz/¼ cup) caster sugar

1 egg

40g (1½oz/generous ¼ cup) plain (all-purpose) flour

½ tsp baking powder

¼ tsp salt

2 Tbsp milk

2 tsp cocoa powder

2 tsp hot water

25g (1oz) dark chocolate, roughly chopped

30g (1oz/1½ Tbsp) dulce de leche, plus extra to swirl

Preheat the oven to 180°C (160°C fan/350°F/gas mark 4) and lightly grease a small skillet or baking dish.

Melt the butter in the microwave or in a small saucepan.

In a bowl, beat together the sugar and egg until combined. Pour in the melted butter and stir until smooth. Mix in the flour, baking powder and salt before stirring in the milk.

In a separate bowl, dissolve the cocoa powder in the hot water to make a thick paste. Add half of the batter mixture to this cocoa bowl and mix until evenly combined. Stir in the chocolate chunks.

Stir the dulce de leche into the other half of the batter.

Add alternating spoonfuls of the batter mixtures into your skillet or dish. Drizzle about a teaspoon of extra dulce de leche on top. Use a skewer to gently swirl the batter a little – don't swirl it too much or the batters will just blend together.

Bake for 17–25 minutes, then remove from the oven and let it cool for a few minutes before diving in.

CHOCOLATE

chocolate & hazelnut millionaire's shortbread

These sweet little squares are a real classic. I remember buying these from the supermarket after school and eating them layer by layer, much to the annoyance of my friends. Nibbling off the milky chocolate, licking the sickly sweet caramel and then ending with my favourite bit, the shortbread. This version is a little more grown up, with a lightly spiced chocolate base and a caramel layer packed with roasted hazelnuts and a generous pinch of sea salt to balance out some of that sweetness.

Makes 9

For the shortbread base

120g (4¼oz/½ cup) cold unsalted butter, diced, plus extra for greasing

150g (5½oz/1 cup plus 2 Tbsp) plain (all-purpose) flour

50g (1¾oz/¼ cup) caster (granulated) sugar

20g (¾oz/3 heaped Tbsp) cocoa powder

½ tsp ground cinnamon

¼ tsp ground cardamom

¼ tsp salt

For the topping

160g (5½oz/1¼ cups) blanched hazelnuts

1 x 397-g (14-oz) can condensed milk

100g (3½oz/½ cup) light brown sugar

125g (4½oz/½ cup plus 1 Tbsp) unsalted butter

1 tsp flaky sea salt

120g (4¼oz) dark chocolate

small handful of cacao nibs (optional)

Preheat the oven to 200°C (180°C fan/400°F/gas mark 6). Grease a 20-cm (8-in) square cake pan and line with baking paper, leaving an overhang that will help you to lift the shortbread out later.

Place all the shortbread ingredients into a bowl. Use your fingertips to rub the diced butter into the dry ingredients until crumbly. Knead and squeeze the dough a few times in the bowl to bring it together in clumps.

Tip the dough into the prepared pan and press it down evenly into all the corners. Use the back of a spoon to smooth it out. Bake for 20–25 minutes until cooked through, then leave to cool completely.

Add the hazelnuts to a baking sheet and roast in the oven for 10 minutes until fragrant and golden. Remove from the oven and let cool before chopping them roughly, leaving a few whole.

To make the caramel, add the condensed milk, sugar, butter and salt to a saucepan. Heat over a medium-low heat until the butter and sugar melt. Stir continuously for 8–12 minutes until the caramel thickens and starts to darken in colour. It's quite easy for the caramel to catch at the bottom of the pan, so be sure to keep stirring, especially in the corners.

Remove from the heat, stir in the hazelnuts to coat and then pour this mixture onto the biscuit base, spreading it in an even layer. Let it cool and firm up for 15 minutes.

Melt the chocolate in the microwave or in a bowl set over a pan of simmering water. Pour the chocolate onto the caramel layer and tilt it about so it covers all the caramel. Top with the cacao nibs (if using). Chill in the refrigerator for 10–15 minutes until set. When it's firm enough to cut, remove from the pan and use a hot knife to cut into neat squares or bars.

buckwheat, sesame & chocolate cookies

This is one for the gluten-free crew, but also for everyone else. Buckwheat is a beautiful flour, bringing an earthy nuttiness and textural interest to whatever it gets incorporated into. If you've never baked with it before, these cookies are a good place to start. They've got just the right amount of chew, with a soft chocolatey interior – a keeper for the cookie jar.

Makes 12

100g (3½oz/scant ½ cup) unsalted butter, softened

50g (1¾oz/¼ cup) caster (granulated) sugar

100g (3½oz/½ cup) light brown sugar

1 egg

130g (4½oz/1 cup) buckwheat flour

2 Tbsp cocoa powder

50g (1¾oz/⅓ cup) jumbo oats

½ tsp bicarbonate of soda (baking soda)

¼ tsp salt

100g (3½oz) milk chocolate, roughly chopped

3 Tbsp sesame seeds

Preheat the oven to 180°C (160°C fan/350°F/gas mark 4). Line two baking sheets with baking paper.

Cream the butter and both sugars together with an electric whisk for 3–5 minutes until pale and creamy, scraping down the sides of the bowl every so often. Add the egg and continue to beat for another minute.

In a separate bowl, mix together the flour, cocoa powder, jumbo oats, bicarbonate of soda and salt. Pour this into the butter mixture and mix on low speed until just combined, then stir in the chopped chocolate. Cover the bowl and chill the dough in the refrigerator for 20 minutes.

Put the sesame seeds into a shallow dish. Use an ice-cream scoop or tablespoon to scoop balls of dough onto the baking sheets. Roll each one in the sesame seeds before placing back on the baking sheets, leaving 2.5cm (1in) of space between them, as they will spread a little.

Bake for 12–14 minutes, or until the edges are set but the middles are still a little soft. Let them cool for a few minutes on the sheets before moving them to a wire rack to cool completely.

index

acknowledgements

Writing a cookbook is a real labour of love. A journey that has you often feeling like you're in it alone but that wouldn't be possible without a wonderful team beside you. My name is on the front but this book came together with the help of some special people.

To Mama Bo, thank you for letting me take over your kitchen to recipe test for days on end while making a huge mess in the process. I've lost count of how much butter, cream and pastry I stored in your fridge because mine was too small but I'll always be grateful!

To the Pyrmont girls, thank you for tasting all the cakes, cookies, desserts and everything in between that I brought home nearly every day, even when we were supposed to be 'cutting back on the sugar'. It was a tough job, but you all stepped up to the challenge.

Thank you to Julia, the best assistant I could have asked for. Thank you for all the last-minute runs to the shop, always keeping calm in the kitchen and for lining those loaf tins so perfectly.

Thank you to Laura for such stunning photography. I was so glad when you agreed to work on this book and you made all the recipes come alive with plenty of laughter along the way. And to Jo for the stretching sessions after long days on our feet.

Thank you to Anna for sourcing the most stunning props. You've got such a good eye and I really appreciated all your comments and suggestions on the shoot days. And thank you for loving custard as much as I do. To the team at Northbank, thank you for all the hard work you've put in over the years. And thank you, Martin, for being such a fab agent.

To the team at Quadrille, thank you for making this book happen! Thanks, Céline, for reaching out and believing in me and making me feel included throughout the whole process. Thank you, Katherine, for the beautiful book design and for going back and forth with me so much!

A big thank you to my wonderful Instagram community. Thank you to the people that get excited to make my recipes as soon as I post them or just send through such kind messages about the bakes that they've tried. The support from around the world continues to blow my mind and I'm so grateful for everyone who has bought a book, shared my work and baked one of my recipes. I look forward to sharing so much more with you all in the future.

And above all, soli Deo gloria.

Publishing Director: Sarah Lavelle
Senior Commissioning Editor: Céline Hughes
Senior Designer: Katherine Keeble
Photographer: Laura Edwards
Food Stylist: Benjamina Ebuehi
Food Stylist Assistant: Julia Aden
Prop Stylist: Anna Wilkins
Head of Production: Stephen Lang
Senior Production Controller: Katie Jarvis

Published in 2022 by Quadrille,
an imprint of Hardie Grant Publishing

Reprinted in 2022
10 9 8 7 6 5 4 3 2

Quadrille
52–54 Southwark Street
London SE1 1UN
quadrille.com

Cataloguing in Publication Data: a catalogue
record for this book is available from the
British Library.

Text © Benjamina Ebuehi 2022
Design © Quadrille 2022
Photography © Laura Edwards 2022

ISBN 978 1 78713 801 8

Printed in China

FSC
www.fsc.org

MIX
Paper from
responsible sources
FSC™ C020056